REVOLUTIONARY

Unique, innovative, and complete in itself, *A Grimoire of Shadows* was developed in 1967 as an alternative to the Gardnerian Tradition, by one of Wicca's greatest Elders. Circulating underground for a quarter century, this classic manual on Witchcraft is only now available to the public.

A thorough introduction to Craft studies, *A Grimoire of Shadows* provides a complete and self-contained system of Magic, a richly developed cycle of seasonal rituals, and an essential guide to starting and operating a coven. A living piece of Craft history, this is the sourcebook for several Wiccan Traditions.

Time-tested and proven, *A Grimoire of Shadows* has been thoroughly researched and contains restored Pagan materials unavailable anywhere else. Learn the true story behind the Pagan Way from one of the founders who wrote many of the original rituals of this legendary organization. Discover a wealth of material on every contingency you might encounter in starting your own coven or beginning on the path of Magical study.

A Grimoire of Shadows is the ultimate reference book for the student of Magic, Paganism, or Witchcraft. Covering every aspect of modern Craft practice, from astral projection and amulets, to herbalism and healing, to making your own coven and starting your own tradition—this is the book of shadows no Witch should be without.

About the Author

Ed Fitch is one of the founders and major scholars of modern Paganism. Initiated into Gardnerian Wicca during the mid-1960s, he has continually added to the existing background lore on Wicca and mainstream Paganism, and is widely considered to be one of the best and most influential writers of rituals in the United States today. His ceremonies are poetic reconstructions of ancient rites in a modern and magical form, using original material researched from historical, anthropological, and literary sources worldwide.

The son of parents from a Russian immigrant community, Ed traveled widely as a boy, living in construction camps in the Southwest desert, mining camps in the West, on a ranch far back in the northern California wilderness, on a farm in Virginia, and on an old southern estate near Washington, D.C. As an Air Force officer, he traveled the world before settling down in a civilian job as an aerospace engineer in Southern California.

To Write to the Author

If you wish to contact the author or would like more information about this book, please write to the author in care of Llewellyn Worldwide, and we will forward your request. Both the author and publisher appreciate hearing from you and learning of your enjoyment of this book and how it has helped you. Llewellyn Worldwide cannot guarantee that every letter written to the author can be answered, but all will be forwarded. Please write to:

Llewellyn Worldwide Ltd.
P.O. Box 64383, Dept. K659-9, St. Paul, MN 55164-0383, U.S.A.
Please enclose a self-addressed, stamped envelope for reply, or $1.00 to cover costs.
If outside the U.S.A., enclose international postal reply coupon.

Free Catalog from Llewellyn

For more than ninety years Llewellyn has brought its readers knowledge in the fields of metaphysics and human potential. Learn about the newest books in spiritual guidance, natural healing, astrology, occult philosophy, and more. Enjoy book reviews, New Age articles, a calendar of events, plus current advertised products and services. To get your free copy of Llewellyn's New Worlds, send your name and address to:

Llewellyn's New Worlds of Mind and Spirit
P.O. Box 64383, Dept. K659-9, St. Paul, MN 55164-0383, U.S.A

A GRIMOIRE OF SHADOWS

OF

SHADOWS

WITCHCRAFT, PAGANISM & MAGIC

ED FITCH

1996
Llewellyn Publications
St. Paul, Minnesota 55164-0383, U.S.A.

FIRST EDITION
Second Printing, 1996

Cover design by Maria Mazzara
Illustrations and cover art by Rick Allendorf
Interior design and editing by Connie Hill

Library of Congress Cataloging-in-Publication Data
Fitch, Ed
    A grimoire of shadows : witchcraft, paganism & magick / Ed Fitch. — 1st ed.
      p.   cm. —

    ISBN 1-56718-659-9 (trade paperback)
    1. Witchcraft. 2. Magic. 3. Paganism. I. Title.
BF1566.F47   1996
133.4'3—dc20
                                   96-16407
                                       CIP

Llewellyn Publications
A Division of Llewellyn Worldwide, Ltd.
St. Paul, Minnesota, 55164-0383, U.S.A.

DEDICATION

To Lillian (1915–1993)

Long ago, mother,
You taught me to revere the wilderness.
In its magnificence,
    Your spirit still abides.

OTHER BOOKS BY THE AUTHOR

The Castle of Deception (Fiction)

Magical Rites from the Crystal Well

The Rites of Odin

CONTENTS

CREDITS

Some of the training material was adapted liberally from the works of the great Austrian magician, Franz Bardon, and some exercises I modified from William Gray. The Handfasting Ceremony incorporates some of Dion Fortune's poetry. The Midsummer Rite includes magical poetry by Robert Graves.

My warmest thanks to my long-time apprentice Silver Tree for his long hours in retyping the vast bulk of this material from the original aging and brittle manuscripts onto modern computer disks. To Noël, who was with me on my earliest adventures. And of course, my deepest thanks to my original mentor on this book a quarter century ago, my good friend Raymond Buckland.

IN THE BEGINNING WAS THE WORD . . .

The time was in the mid-part of the year 1967. I had been initiated into Gardnerian Wicca a few months earlier, following several years of searching and solitary, intensive study on my own. I was in the military at that time, and whenever I could get a weekend free from my duties at Hanscom Air Force Base in Massachusetts I would catch a plane down to Long Island to visit and to share stimulating conversation and soul-satisfying Magical rites with my new friends there.

Ray Buckland and his wife Rosemary had been in the United States for several years, sent here by the coven of the late Gerald Gardner. As I understood it, they were half-seriously given the task of being "missionaries to carry Wicca to the wayward colonies of the New World." (I am certain that Lady Olwen and the rest of the Witches on the Isle of Man could never have dreamed how enormously successful this small mission would ultimately be!) The Bucklands were my mentors and best friends, and my visits were always memorable.

On this one Saturday morning, however, I arrived from the airport to find them both dejected and angry. Upon asking a few questions I learned that one of their newer initiates had, against the rules, copied out a fair portion of the Book of Shadows, added some Quabalah to it, and was now loudly proclaiming that she was the Grand High Priestess of the United States and Canada, of a totally new branch of Witchcraft! (And she did have some very valid material.) The geographic claim had no basis of course, but the television networks, news magazines, and newspapers loved it! This was the late 1960s, remember, and the Age of Aquarius was in full flower.

Rosemary served tea, but the usual outrageous, ebullient, and deep conversation still failed to manifest itself. The mood was just too low, and the silent periods were long.

I cleared my throat. "Ray ... Rosemary ... I have an idea. It's something that I've been working on for some time." (I hadn't, really, but they didn't know that.) "As you know, I've been immersing myself in Dion Fortune's writings for the last several years, and she has this interesting concept of an Outer Court. It's a system for training new candidates without giving them any of the inner, secret lore … "

Quickly, I sketched out my idea. Under the Bucklands' close supervision I would research and assemble a very simple and short training system with rituals that generally paralleled those of Gardnerian Wicca, but which used none of the secret material or methods. It could be used for training and evaluating new people without putting the Book of Shadows at risk.

This was the beginning of the "Outer Court" books, now formally published for the first time as one volume, A *Grimoire of Shadows*, by Llewellyn Publications. I had never intended for it to be copyrighted or published: it was, like the Pagan Way materials (written a couple years later), designed to be a set of volumes to be passed around from coven to coven to candidates in an "underground" manner. The spirit of the late sixties was ostensibly one of selflessly working "for the people." Like millions of others, I felt at the time that this was to be the wave of the future. Maybe it's because I'm older now, but I don't think I would be so idealistic if I were to do it again.

Very often since, the "Outer Court Book of Shadows" and the "Grimoire of the Shadows" have been published in parts and sections by others who were perhaps a bit more pragmatic than I. The material has been incorporated into "witchcraft-by-mail" courses, narrated in readings on series of tapes distributed in England, and as major parts of books with a variety of people claiming authorship or permission to publish. I've seen portions of the rituals quoted in novels, and even in at least one role-playing game! It has given me pause when I hear that various groups here and there cherish their own modified, hand-copied versions as "an ancient Celtic (or other) tradition, passed down from generation to generation."

Returning to Massachusetts, I eagerly began the task. For four years I had been methodically working my way through the exercises in Bardon's *Initiation Into Hermetics* as well as studying William Gray, Dion Fortune, and Doreen Valiente. I am an inveterate note-taker, and the contents of my spiral-bound workbooks were transcribed into a Grimoire of Magical lore and some training techniques.

I had read Graves' *The White Goddess* and his compelling novel *Watch the North Wind Rise*, Frasier's *The Golden Bough*, and as much Germanic and Celtic and Greek mythology as I could find. I had a treasure-trove of history, archaeology, and anthropology books that I had purchased in Denmark and Germany a few years before, and a thick file of research notes taken from obscure sources in the Library of Congress in Washington, D.C.

In rapid order the Grimoire grew to twenty and then thirty pages of training material, with the promise of expanding to more than twice that length before it would be completed. The rituals looked good but very different from the Magical training exercises, and it became apparent that they would have to be part of yet a second Outer Court book. And there would be a lot of these rituals!

I was fascinated by the legends and literature of pre-Classical Greece, and by the enigmatic, beautiful, and sensual Goddess art of ancient Crete. Pagan Ireland and Britain seemed to be lands of eternal sunrise where song and poetry were the purest Magic. Iron-Age Germany was a land of austere, powerful Magics and an archetypal sense of honor that would outlast even the Gods themselves. As background, I remembered the wild, primal magnificence and mystery of the remote California mountain wilderness where I had lived as a boy. Through it all was woven Robert Graves' vision of the Language of Myth and Legend.

In spare moments during my workdays or on a flight I would jot down notes, concepts, and ideas. Each morning back in Massachusetts I would get up an hour earlier than usual and type out another couple pages of ritual or of psychic exercises while watching the sun rise through the New England forest.

The Bucklands, bless them, examined all my work and told me what would be usable and what wouldn't. Then I would hop the next plane back to Boston and continue this work which so absorbed my free time.

World events intruded. The military sent me first to Vietnam, and then to the jungles of Thailand. My writing became tempered by the traditions of these exotic countries and their fascinating people, the ever-present sounds of war, the tensions of being in constant danger, and the mixture of excitement and fear when actually under fire. (My psychic senses became accurate beyond all expectations when I was being shot at!) I had taken a couple of my best reference books with me and continued my writing and revisions as time and the war permitted. Surprisingly, I got a lot done!

I had heard that those of us who served in the war zone would be given our preference in assignments when we got back to the United States. I had asked for a research assignment in Florida, so with that unerring precision for which the military is famous, I received orders for North Dakota.

By this time both the *Outer Court Book of Shadows* and the *Grimoire of the Shadows* were finished. (There were to be revisions in coming years, but they were fairly close to the formally published version which you now hold.)

During all this time I kept up an extensive correspondence with a number of people interested in the Craft. On frequent Air Force business trips around the country I was able to take side trips to visit many of these good people. When visiting, I often performed initiations into the new Outer Court for those whom I felt had little chance of finding and working with an established coven.

My initial concept for the Outer Court was that the materials could be widely and openly shared. I had reckoned without human nature. Each time I performed the initiations and presented a set of the two volumes to the new Priestess and Priest, the books immediately went into wall safes, behind hidden panels, or into steel strongboxes.

There was clearly a need for something new to supplement the Outer Court. I had a good bit of time on my hands and it was obvious that something straight-forward and suitable for those new to the Old Religion should be written for pub-lic distribution. The North Dakota winter set in, with its usual, unremitting arctic winds and Siberian temperatures. Working from my notes and my library I began assembling and writing the Pagan Way materials as something of a parallel but more open system.

A brief digression may be in order at this point. At that time I was working via mail and telephone with my friend "Thomas" in Philadelphia, publishing the original *The Waxing Moon* newsletter (which we soon renamed *The Crystal Well*, per agreement with the publication's original founder). We decided to set up one mailing center in Minot and another in Philadelphia, sending out sets of the Pagan Way materials to anyone who requested them, asking only for donations to help defray the cost of mailing. Further, we requested suggestions and comments from those who received our mailings.

The first rituals were sent out, and the replies were enthusiastic, with a fre-quent, rather wistful request that we perhaps should have foreseen. Many of our correspondents wrote that they were isolated solitaries, out in the empty Great Plains or in suburbs where they knew no one with like interests. Group rites were wonderful, but did we have any solitary seasonal and Magical rituals? I went back, assembled and wrote a full system of parallel solitary Pagan Way rituals. These became the most popular of all that we released!

More and more Pagan Way mailing centers were set up, others began pub-lishing them individually or in groups, and the whole thing began spreading rapidly. Again, it was an idealistic era, and all this material was provided free of copyright to whoever wanted it. Reproduction and further distribution was encouraged. Perhaps I should have copyrighted it, but ... well, it was another time and another place.

In the meantime, use of the Outer Court continued to grow.

I underestimated the system at first. On a trip to New York City I visited with the late Susan Roberts to help her on a book about Wicca that she was writing. While there I met her friend Joe Lukach, himself of a Caribbean tradition some-what similar to Santeria. Joe examined the copy that I had given him, then gave me a bit of a quizzical look.

"Ed," he said, "What you've written is a full tradition in itself. Didn't you real-ize that?" Well, I hadn't. It added a new dimension to the possibilities for the Outer Court, something that, first, I hadn't really considered and second, by this time the control of the Outer Court was already out of my hands since it was spreading on its own anyway!

An actual bit of history might be useful here—as best as I can reconstruct it. The original Gardnerian coven in Louisville, Kentucky had received many queries about Witchcraft, and they responded with letters of guidance and suggested reading lists. In particular, there were some correspondents in the Carolinas and Georgia who were intelligent and diligent. After a while these good people began wanting more actual Craft lore.

In the past I had given my friends in the Louisville Coven copies of my Pagan Way and Outer Court materials. (There weren't very many of us in those days, and we kept in close touch with each other.) Packages of the Pagan Way materials, were sent to them from Louisville, and the Southerners used it for themselves and for other new people who came to them.

Another year or so and they were ready for more, so Outer Court initiations were given to them. A growing number of Outer Court covens began springing up, while the Pagan Way groves continued to spread as yet more students came in.

It became obvious a year or two later that it was time for Gardnerian initiations, and these covens were established in the Carolinas and Georgia. Also, there seemed to have been some cross-fertilization from other Wiccan traditions. Meanwhile, the Outer Court continued to spread even farther as individual Witches, not yet quite ready for Gardnerian (or other tradition) initiation moved away and took copies of the books with them. In some cases, Priestesses and Priests used the Outer Court materials as a core around which to build their own eclectic but very effective traditions.

Like ripples spreading from where a rock is dropped in a quiet pond, the Pagan Way and the Outer Court, followed after a time by Gardnerian and other traditions, have kept on expanding, doubling and redoubling, as more and more people have come into them from the outside. Nowadays, yearly Pagan festivals in North Carolina, South Carolina, and Georgia draw thousands to their gatherings. Long ago I lost track of who was involved and what was happening and how, but I couldn't be happier about it!

My theory is that neo-Paganism and Wicca satisfy an archetypally-deep craving that everyone has for an archaic Magic that works, provides mystery that pierces far beyond the mundane, a glamor that inspires and fascinates, and fosters a deep religious sense of devotion that goes beyond all time and space.

A leavening of the Old Ways does good for society. It can replace widespread ennui and bitterness about the artificiality, hypocrisy, and manipulativeness that seem so all-pervading today. Paganism can act as a "societal antibiotic" saving this country and others from regional breakup, civil/interracial war, and anarchy.

If, in spite of it all, the very worst happens and societal collapse does indeed come about, then the back-to-life's-fundamentals-and-use-what-science-offers mindset of today's Pagans will aid enormously (they are a highly intelligent group of people from the start). It will help our folk to survive and provide a nucleus around which something far better can be built in the times to come.

This satisfies me greatly since I have always been something of a crusader, with an eye to the future. If I was born a century too soon to pilot a starship and explore the Infinite Frontier, then at least I can provide solid foundations of life for those who ultimately will do so!

Now and then, at a Pagan gathering up in the mountains, I will be enjoying myself in the company of kindred souls, perhaps with a tankard of ale. There will be an announcement that a handfasting will take place, and all are welcome to attend. I will go, of course, since I like such things. Usually I watch from a place out in the trees toward the back of the crowd

The bride will be radiant and beautiful, as are all brides, and the groom smiling, strong and handsome, as are all grooms. The ceremony begins, and the liturgy begins sounding familiar.

I realize that, although the rite has been modified somewhat, the words are mine. I wrote the original rite!

I look at the bride and the groom. Their faces show the happiness of a joining that will link them for years, or perhaps for a lifetime. I look at the people around them, smiling or in tears of joy. *I've done something good for someone*, I think to myself. *They'll probably never know that I forged the link that joins them, but I know it. I've given them something worthwhile, and that's what matters, after all!*

I raise my tankard of ale toward them in silent salute, and then settle comfortably at the base of an oak tree, out in back at the edge of the woods, to watch the proceedings.

The feeling is good. Very good.

Ed Fitch
Orange County, California
Fall 1994

THE ROAD BEGINS*

In the name of the Lady, we give you greetings…

Two types of seekers will be using this book. Perhaps after long and due consideration you have been selected to enter the Outer Court of Witchcraft. The Elders and members of a coven have examined your qualifications, and studied you as a person. Perhaps you are not in the ancient Craft as yet, and must still be examined in many ways, both visible and invisible. In the meantime the Elders think it is wise that you commence the study of Magic, and begin reading some of the literature and history which pertains to the Craft.

Or perhaps you are already an initiate of Wicca, and wish to expand your understanding and your powers. You may have heard of this Book and decided to follow its curriculum.

Wherever you are on the Path toward the Mysteries, proceed at the training and reading at a pace which is comfortable to you, and think it over carefully as you go along … for when you finish you will be a very different person.

The occult training delineated in the following pages does not include any of the secret lore and ritual of Witchcraft, for these are secret and protected by the strongest of oaths. What follows is instead a related form of "ritual Magic," mixed with Wiccan folk Magic, which conditions and trains the mind and body, and which after a time can grant you some rather substantial powers.

A fair warning though … the psychic training exercises (if done in series and properly) will take a considerable amount of time, since you will be involved in opening the psychic centers and conditioning the subconscious. You can expect subjective results in only a few days of close training, accomplish small or subtle phenomena within two to four weeks of training, and in six months or a year you may be doing some major and rather striking things.

The work herein has been used by Witches and other students of the Mysteries for a long time … indeed, for decades. The Magic you will be practicing is strong and fully in consonance with the Magic of the Craft.

Continue onward … and may the blessings of the Old Ones go with you!

PART I

LORE

To Know, To Dare, To Will,
To Keep Silent
Are the four words of the Magus.
In order to Dare, we must Know,
In order to Will, we must Dare,
We must Will to possess Empire
To reign, we must
Keep Silent.

The Craft of the Ancients

Witchcraft is the most ancient religion known to the human race. Its origins are incredibly archaic; members of the Craft can pick out portions of recognizable rites, as performed today, on cave wall-paintings twenty-five millennia old, and it is said that a few—a very few—covens have written records that go back nearly that distance in time. Traces and portions of Magical tools and Witches' amulets have been found in deposits a hundred thousand years old.

There are legends within the Craft that our very distant forebears worshipped the Goddess and the Horned God in jewelled and spired cities whose names have been forgotten for tens of thousands of years, and rich lands of mighty green mountains and golden plains ... all swallowed beneath the seas long ages ago. Yet in these cities and these forests men and women loved and worked, danced, laughed, and cried; some of their blood still flows in our veins.

The Craft of the Wise Ones is probably as old as humankind itself, and so deeply ingrained in human nature that it is a part of all that we call "human." Even those who in this life know nothing of what is called Witchcraft will still in their own way repeat the legends behind the Rites of Love, Birth, and Death. They will still partake of Magic in a warm, sunlit forest, sense the more-than-physical life power of a raging thunderstorm, and on still, moonlit nights will cause strange things to happen which they themselves will not believe in days to follow.

No one living can plot out a complete, or even general history of the Craft; it vanishes into the mists of distant prehistory, at one time reigning supreme over all of humankind, at times sharing men's hearts with its various daughter religions and, on occasion, persecuted by the ignorant and hidden underground. Witchcraft has the deepest roots, and inevitably rises again to be as it was in times past. We are now in such an era of renascent growth and strength, as many do seek the spiritual and emotional richness of Wicca, and the ancient lore of wisdom and the rites are drawn together once more for the benefit of all.

This book is such a collection of Witch-lore. The traditions and rituals are reconstructed from fragments, portions, and shards that have survived the harsh centuries, carefully restored to be as they once were in ages past. A vast amount of material still remains, and will be added as it is made ready.

According to the most ancient traditions, the lore of the Inner Court must remain a close secret, being entrusted only to those who have been carefully examined and cross-checked, and who have served a long probationary period. Some Inner Court materials have been published, though the true core of

Witchcraft will doubtless never be in print for reasons which are obvious to the various Elders, but which are too complex to explain here.

Much of the Outer Court has been available in small and usually unconnected fragments through literary and historical sources. A generally lesser degree of secrecy may be maintained for the Outer Court. Those who have a deep interest in being accepted into the Craft of the Witches may more readily be accepted into the Outer Court, and thus be on the path to the Secrets.

The quest begins here. To the true seeker is given the blessing:

> *Go ye ever in the Path of the Gods,*
> *Seek always the Truth,*
> *And Blessed Be!*

The Lost Heritage of the Elder Races

Our kind is not the first to live on the green earth, and it shall not be the last. There have been civilizations of which we have no knowledge which have vanished with hardly a trace. In time, we shall follow them, for we are related to more than merely those of humankind. The legends of the Old Religion say that "Single is the race of Gods and men, and from a single source we both draw breath." The Gods are our kin; so also are the Elder Ones—for at length it becomes impossible to separate one from the other.

It is given to each race to have this world for a while—to learn and to progress upward toward a finer plane; then, when sufficient development and sufficient wisdom is attained, to depart for another realm of existence, leaving behind their lands and works for a newer, less-developed people to try to understand and attempt to use. We do not know how many earlier races there have been, only that some were non-human and pre-human. Ancient lore speaks of the Tuatha de Damnu, the Tuatha de Danaan, and those whom we call Elven or Faery.

The worlds to which the Elder races ascend are superior in every way to this world of ours. They are places of beauty, of Magic, of mystery, of brilliant and joyous color. Life goes on there, and all manner of normal events, though on a higher level of existence. Death also exists, though its meanings and imports are not so dread as here—being merely an intermediate change in lives, throughout which consciousness and memory is retained. All of the arts and sciences, love, and even love-making are far more compelling and enthralling in those far regions.

Transition to the Otherworlds is made by Magic of the mind. The one making it becomes insubstantial, invisible, then vanishes altogether from the perception of the earthbound. Returns are possible, but become less and less likely. This Magic method is said to be known to the highest adepts of the Craft.

The method for this transition, however, generally must be sought out and gained by the individuals, for it involves not just surface knowledge, but a deep understanding within the very depths of the soul. It cannot fully be written, and is not easily passed between people by any normal means.

One seeking this manner of transformation is advised to study the lore of the Elven Folk, who are perhaps the closest to us and of whom some knowledge yet remains. The ways are of moonlight and forest, silent meadows and mists, of candles and firelight, and the Magic of being "between the worlds." Myth and legend have the keys, and the practice of spells and Magics will condition the mind and the body for the change.

~

The Witch's Rede of Chivalry

Insofar as the Craft of the Wise is the most ancient and most honorable creed of humankind, it behooves all who are Witches to act in ways that give respect to the Old Gods, to their sisters and brothers of the Craft, and to themselves. Therefore, be it noted that:

1. Chivalry is a high code of honor which is of most ancient Pagan origin, and must be lived by all who follow the Old Ways.

2. It must be kenned that thoughts and intent put forth on this Middle-Earth will wax strong in other worlds beyond, and return—bringing into creation, on this world, that which had been sent forth. Thus one should exercise discipline, for "as ye do plant, so shall ye harvest."

3. It is only by preparing our minds to be as Gods that we can ultimately attain godhead.

4. "This above all ... to thine own self be true ..."

5. A Witch's word must have the validness of a signed and witnessed oath. Thus, give your word sparingly, and adhere to it like iron.

6. Refrain from speaking ill of others, for not all truths of the matter may be known.

7. Pass not unverified words about another, for hearsay is, in large part, a thing of falsehoods.

8. Be thou honest with others, and have them know that honesty is likewise expected of them.

9. The fury of the moment plays folly with the truth; to keep one's head is a virtue.

10. Contemplate always the consequences of thine acts upon others. Strive not to harm.

11. Diverse covens may well have diverse views on love between members and with others. When a coven, clan, or grove is visited or joined, one should discern quietly their practices, and abide thereby.

12. Dignity, a gracious manner, and a good humor are much to be admired.

13. As a Witch, thou hast power, and thy powers wax strongly as wisdom increases. Therefore exercise discretion in the use thereof.

14. Courage and honor endure forever. Their echoes remain when the mountains have crumbled to dust.

15. Pledge friendship and fealty to those who so warrant it. Strengthen others of the Brethren and they shall strengthen thee.

16. Thou shalt not reveal the secrets of another Witch or another Coven. Others have laboured long and hard for them, and cherish them as treasures.

17. Though there may be differences between those of the Old Ways, those who are once-born must see nothing, and must hear nothing.

18. Those who follow the Mysteries should be above reproach in the eyes of the world.

19. The laws of the land should be obeyed whenever possible and within reason, for in the main they have been chosen with wisdom.

20. Have pride in thyself, and seek perfection in body and in mind. For the Lady has said, "How canst thou honor another unless thou give honor to thyself first?"

21. Those who seek the Mysteries should consider themselves as select of the Gods, for it is they who shall lead the race of humankind to the highest of thrones and beyond the very stars.

Order of Rank Within the Outer Court of the Craft

The spiritual head of each coven shall be the Priestess. She shall be pleasing of face, spirit, and soul, bearing always in mind that she is the representative of the Goddess, and that in the working of ritual and Magic the Lady shines through her eyes and speaks with her tongue. She must be gracious, fair, and merciful, yet with a fire and a confidence before which nothing can stand. Magic to her should be a way of life, and she should constantly be studying all things dealing with Magic and the Craft. She may choose whomsoever she pleases as her priest, though he too should be skilled in Magic.

The Priest is responsible for the administration of the coven, and for all the mundane but necessary matters of organization required for the group. He works on an equal basis with the Priestess. He must be fair, impartial, strong in will and body, with a wide knowledge of Magic and of the world. He is the representative of the God, and while working ritual and Magic the Horned One sees through his eyes and speaks with his tongue. Magic and science should be a way of life with him, and he should study all things related to the Craft. Power and confidence are his hallmarks.

Although theoretically the Priestess should be the absolute head of the coven, either the Priestess or the Priest may in actuality be the *de facto* leader, depending on which has the greater background in learning, psychic training, experience in things Magical, and ability and charisma in dealing with people.

If the numbers of a coven grow to exceed thirteen, or if the distance to the coven's meeting place (covenstead) is too long for convenience, or if there be some difference of opinion to warrant it, any coven may divide to form another coven. The Priestess and Priest of the new coven shall be chosen by the members thereof. If they do not already have the *Book of Shadows of the Outer Court* and the *Grimoire of the Shadows* (Author's note: here combined into one volume), it shall be the responsibility of the Priestess of the mother coven to see that the new group receives a copy of each. The Priestess and Priest of the mother coven will see that the new group has properly consecrated Magical tools. The mother group will provide advice, Magical help, communications with other groups, and other good offices. The new coven, in return, will pledge fealty to the Priestess of the mother coven.

When one is initiated into the Inner Court it is important that the initiate keep quite separate the rituals, Magic, and secrets of the Inner and Outer Courts, respectively.

It is preferred that the Priestess of the coven be referred to as "Lady _____," especially if her Craft name is used. This title signifies implicitly her connection with the Goddess.

Forest Magic

When the rites are regularly performed in a wooded place, especially one which is remote, it will "come alive" in both obvious and subtle ways. Growing things will prosper, and wild animals will find the area pleasing, appearing in greater numbers. Witches and those who are even slightly sensitive psychically will soon observe that there is a definite "charge" or aura about the vicinity, and often wood-sprites and other elementals will be seen—first at night and later even by day. This is the type of "enchanted woodland" mentioned in many ancient legends.

The Craft as a Religion of Life

From the most ancient times Witchcraft was a religion of birth, fertility, and rebirth. In those early days, much of our time with the Gods was spent in assuring that the crops would grow high, the beasts of the field would prosper, and that strong, wise children would be born to those of the coven. Though they may come again, those times are past—for the world has changed.

The mystery, the joy, and the Magic of our Craft shall ever be with us: though there is no longer a great need for fertility, there is now especially a deep need to truly live! The truth of Witchcraft remains always the same; in the old days a material fruitfulness was needed for life, but now the craving is for fruitfulness within the soul itself.

So, while it is said that the ancient Craft was a fertility religion and the modern Craft a vitality religion, the truth is that it is *both*—yet ever unchanged.

Study of Defensive and Martial Combative Arts

The world is not a peaceful or tranquil place, and it is seldom prudent to fully trust outsiders—even those appointed by the Law—with the safety of oneself, one's family, or those of one's coven. All should be encouraged to take some training in Karate, Hapkido, Judo, Ninjitsu, Aikido, Tai Chi, Kung Fu, or other such martial arts which have a strong (if subtle) metaphysical and Magical philosophy behind them. In addition to keeping the body strong and healthy (which is necessary for Magical training and practice), as well as pleasing to the sight, these activities also quickly build the self-confidence which is so necessary in Magic, and provide intensive basic training in bringing forth the power of the elements.

It is said that semi-Magical combative arts of this sort were common in Europe as late as the early Iron Age, and it is known that weapons and some specialized fighting techniques had a similar metaphysical background. However, it is likely that these were lost during the ages since, particularly with the reign of the Christians.

Also, considering the unfortunate condition of today's civilization, Witches should consider learning about and using modern weapons and techniques which are available. The deer and the rabbit have used non-violence against the wolf and the panther since time immemorial: it does not seem to have done them much good.

Concerning Silence and Discretion

Although the Craft is a religion of joy, mystery, and beauty, in this time we are still few, and there are many to whom, in their ignorance, we cannot truly speak. Though a Witch may have the wisdom of millennia, there is often a vast gulf to cross in even speaking to those of one's own family, and far greater yet is the difficulty of touching the mind and heart of an acquaintance or a stranger. As one of the Craft, you should never press esoteric matters on those who will not receive them, no matter how deeply you may feel, for in doing so, you may not only fail to convince, but may yourself lose psychically and Magically by their ignorant unbelief.

Wait instead for them to be prepared within themselves: to feel the Lady's call, and ask knowledge of you. Time is always on the side of the Witch, and small bits of wisdom from time to time are far more valuable than a long and involved speech at one sitting.

Be always on guard for imposters, for there are many who, for their own advantage, will claim to be Witches. To avoid deception, take no one at their first word; show them hospitality and friendly conversation, but test them in many subtle ways concerning their knowledge, their attitudes, their ways of thinking. Do not take them into your confidence until you are sure that they are true and worthy servants of the Lady.

In the present age we have strength in secrecy, and wisdom grows strong in silence.

~

Accepting New Members into the Craft

It is a basic precept of the Craft that we never go out and solicit new members. On the contrary, a Witch always waits for the seekers to come; those who feel the call will find their own way. Some will be referred to you and will visit in person, others will be brought by friends who know you, and others yet will write; pay personal attention to all and answer their questions as far as your oaths will permit (or less, as you see fit.)

Be genial and relaxed, if speaking to them in person, but question and test them in many subtle ways under the guise of casual conversation and philosophical discussions. Search out not only what they know, but especially what their feelings and attitudes are: what is the reason that this person is interested in Witchcraft? Those who come looking for an easy way to money, sex, and drugs are to be strongly avoided.

~

As the Outside World Sees You

Those who become interested in occultism in general, and Witchcraft in particular, usually wonder at first just what they should say about it to their friends, relatives, and neighbors. The best rule is silence.

The world today is still ignorant of things psychic, and has no understanding of the Craft. Rather than fight the cynicism of unbelief, let your powers grow in quiet, for they will thus become all the stronger.

Of course, one who lives in the spiritual company of the Lady will change as a person, and in time, this will be noticed more and more by those nearby. You should plan some standard approaches in conversation, either profound or witty, for the time when you must make some answer, and either fend off a question, or, if you feel that the questioner may have a serious interest, very carefully lead him or her on to explore their attitudes further.

The following may suggest some good conversational approaches and "outs":

"ESP? Yes, Dr. Rhine at Duke University has made a rather interesting case for it, statistically at any rate. Have you read any of his works?"

"Those pictures and statuettes? I'm interested in anthropology, and these are said to be related to some ancient religion ..."

"Witchcraft? I did some reading in that at one time. The few good books on the subject are by Gardner, Murray, and such. Anthropologists now think it really was a religion, and not a bad one at all ..."

"I know a bit about occultism. I had a spell a few years back when I was quite interested in that sort of thing. Did a lot of reading ..."

Conducting the Rites

The best and most powerful method of conducting the rituals of the Craft is for the Priestess and the Priest to have thoroughly memorized each ceremony and all its words. The words and thoughts of each rite are of great strength, and should be intoned with all appropriate force, power, and dignity. Voice quality and bearing of the Priestess and Priest are strongly Magical.

Even if some of the lines must be read, it should always be remembered that the Priestess is to identify herself *entirely* with the Goddess, and the Priest to become one with the God.

In any Rite, when the coven has lines to speak, it is proper for the Priestess and/or Priest to prompt the group if such is necessary.

When a Witch has become quite experienced at performing ceremonies, she or he will know what is to be said, and speak the words spontaneously without need of a script. This inspired and knowledgeable means of performing rituals is the best of all.

Adding to the Books

The "Book of Shadows" and the "Grimoire of Shadows" (gathered here into one book) are living books to which suitable rites, spells, and exercises should be added as they are deemed worthy and useful. Each coven will have its own needs and interests, and the Books should be augmented to completely fulfill the needs of the Witches. The Priestess and the Priest shall be responsible for the approval and addition of suitable training material, exercises, historical rituals, and so on. It may be useful to consider writing key personal material in alphabets such as Ogham or the Runes for security. It has been said before, but I repeat: the books should only be used by those within the Coven.

~

Training

The Priestess and the Priest shall be responsible for the training of all the coven members, to see that they get the proper guidance in their practice of the Magical arts, and that new approaches such as divination, herbs, and the like are pointed out to them. A personal interest should be taken in the advancement of each person in the coven.

Control Within the Circle

Overall, the Priestess shall be the final authority, since she is the direct representative of the Goddess. However, the Priest or Priestess who is performing the ceremonies of the evening will have the responsibility for controlling and directing those within the circle, and assuring that all within the ritual area are strongly focused on the matter at hand.

Pairing of Men and Women

If it is at all possible, each Witch shall work in the rites with one of the opposite sex, for Magic worked by a man and a woman is the strongest, most powerful type possible. The male-female relationship is one of the most immense depth, complexity, and subtlety, and should be studied carefully by all: the balance between positive and negative, between animus and anima, between yin and yang are all fundamental to Magic. The Great Circle must always have at least one man if the rest be women, or one woman if the rest be men. The Small Circles may be conducted by women alone, or men alone.

When Persecution Threatens

It is usually wise to be prudent in letting others know of your ties with the Craft. Friends will understand and have respect for your convictions, and indeed may well have much interest, but strangers may not comprehend, or may wrongly interpret our creed. Indeed, those who are blind zealots will prefer, without knowing anything of you or your beliefs, to impute the worst possible motives to you and name you as an agent of their devil. Discussing the matter with them is useless, for they usually prefer only to repeat their rote doctrines.*

Although in most cases older Christian adults will not be destructive, those who are younger may at times feel they can show their righteousness by harassment and by destruction of your property. If this seems probable, it is wise to secure your home and belongings by the best possible means and defend them, and yourself, with a strong arm and all the force that is required within the limits of the law. You may wish to call law officers, for they can give much protection, but use care, for in this decaying era laws are being passed which tend to protect the guilty and penalize the innocent. Be certain of your ground.

Always endeavor to be on good terms with those about you, for the best means of overcoming persecution is to avoid it from the beginning. Have genial relationships with your neighbors and especially with the young people in your neighborhood.

Dealing with the Bad Seed

The Priestess and Priest of each coven are responsible for all those whom they initiate, and thus are responsible for instructing their initiates as to what is right and what is wrong. It is wrong to turn onto the Left-Hand-Path, and this must be stressed to all. Anyone who profanes the traditions and writings of the Craft must know that full karmic retribution is inevitable.

If one joins the Craft to later place Craft secrets before the uninitiated, or publicly to offer Witch services or initiations for money, then by Magical means this must be stopped, and by Magical means the guilty one must do penance.

---

* "One can reason with ignorance, but it is futile to argue with stupidity."

Discussion with those who seem borderline in their attitudes is important., and those doing so should use good judgment in dealing with them.

> *When the water stinks*
> *I must break the dam.*
> *In Love I break it...*
> Robert Graves

~

Wyvern Covens

In troubled times it may be that the members of the Craft, and their friends, may be put in peril by flood, by fire, by storm, by riots, by those to whom Life means so little—who strike by darkness. In times when such danger threatens, one or several covens may work together to form a Wyvern Coven.

A Wyvern coven is composed of those who are young, especially those who are just coming of age. These young people are especially strong at Magic, with a natural talent that frequently surpasses the level that usually comes after years of training. Young Witches between the ages of twelve and twenty can thus be formed into a Wyvern, or Dragon Coven, to meet emergencies with a vastly powerful Magic.

When a common danger threatens, the Elders, the Priestesses, and the Priests shall meet and determine by a vote to establish a Wyvern Coven. Such a coven would consist of no more than twelve young Witches, half female, half male, who would work as a team and in pairs. The most beautiful and most magnetic young woman shall act as the Priestess, and the most comely, dynamic young man shall act as the Priest. All would be intensely trained in Magic by their seniors, with the Priest and Priestess receiving the most intense training of all. If any in the group show notable talent, beyond the others, then these especially talented Witches will accede to the Priest or Priestess-ship by the end of the training.

When as much reading, tutoring, and training as time permits has been accomplished and the members are deemed ready by the spokesman of the Elders, the Wyvern Coven shall be provided with its Magical tools and charged formally with its task. No further advice or direction or training will be given any member of the Wyvern Coven unless requested by the Wyvern Priestess or Priest. If Magical or physical aid or backup are requested, the Mother Covens will grant it immediately.

When the tasks of the Wyvern Coven have at last been completed, the young members may elect to keep their coven together. This is their prerogative.

Amulets and Charms

An amulet or talisman is an object which has been especially consecrated to be either a storing-place of power or a nexus-point through which natural powers are drawn to accomplish some goal.

There are many ways whereby a Witch can have protection or aid. The athame is a powerful tool, and if carried, always exerts a good influence about the owner, either for safety or for overcoming personal obstacles.

The Rite of Knots may be performed for any purpose desired, and the knotted cord either carried or worked into some part of one's clothing.

To cure a cold or some other minor illness, a Witch may buy it from the subject for some small sum of money, and immediately knot a string to "tie in the sickness." The string should then be hung on a bush or buried in some remote place where weather, earth, and the elements will eventually moulder it away.

It is frequently most useful to create talismans which can be carried or worn. These can be of any natural material, and should always be fashioned by hand. Oval or circular-shaped amulets are best. Hardwood, copper, brass or silver are materials of particular value in absorbing and holding the spells chanted over them. (If silver from a coin is used, an exorcism should first be performed, for

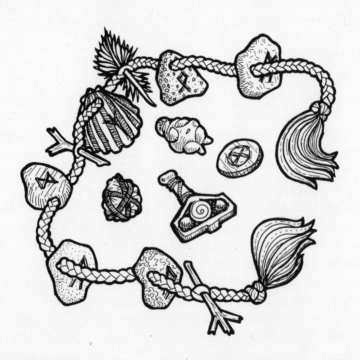

money frequently has gained the wrong sort of psychic loading.) Silver is, of all metals, the best to use for Magical purposes.

It is very important in making a charm or talisman to always bear in mind the purpose for which it is to be used. If your emotions concerning the matter are strong, then so much the better.

Although traditional designs are usually utilized, the Witch may desire to use some sort of "compressed consciousness." To do this, the entire intent of the amulet to be fashioned and all the goals associated with it should be fully written out. The Witch should then rewrite it to half its length, condensed, and yet sacrificing little or no meaning. This being done, the written intent should be again rewritten and further condensed to yet half of this length. The process should be repeated again and again until only a single word, or perhaps only a symbol, remains; to the Witch this one cypher will tell the entire story and all its meanings. This final word or symbol should then be carefully scribed on a disc of silver or copper and consecrated in one of the basic or elaborate rites of the Craft.

Any writing on a charm or talisman should always be in one of the Magical alphabets. The "Tree Alphabet" is one of particular value, though many Witches prefer to use one of the several Runic systems. Both of these alphabets are given elsewhere in this book.

In making talismans for oneself or for others, it is important to search out just what the true needs are which must be fulfilled: does one want money, or is it really a need for security? Is a new job needed, or does a person just need to adjust to his present work? Is a talisman for love desired, or for sexual attraction? If the Witch can get near the true meanings, or the intent behind the meanings, results will come much more quickly and much more accurately.

Very ancient designs from Goddess-worshipping civilizations seem to have a particular strength when used for talismans. Designs from ancient Crete are very useful, as are those from Celtic Gaul, prehistoric Northern Europe, and Bronze Age Briton, Irish, and Welsh motifs. Patterns and pictures from Egypt, Mesopotamia, and Greece should be chosen with care, for in these civilizations there was, after a while, some tampering with the Old Religion and substituting of a god or gods for the Goddess.

The following are some of the designs and uses to which they have been put to since long before the dawn of our present history:

An *equal-armed cross within a disc* is to be used for matters requiring forces from all the elements, or for spiritual sun-power drawn through the Horned God.

Spirals are used for spells dealing with the life-forces.

Linked spirals are used for matters which are karmic in origin, or which at least recur from life to life.

A *stylized willow or vine motif, possibly bound about by a circle*, is to be used when natural forces or serenity of the mind is involved.

In working with the Lady, pentacles, crescents, water, and the triple-circle are useful. Groupings of three or five have special significance.

It is recommended that the Witch make extensive studies of ancient art motifs and apply them to talismans, robes, et cetera. It should be remembered that the symbols from one geographical area are best suited to drawing on the Forces from that area and strengthening that part of the Witch that is linked to these ancient heritages by interest, inclination, or from past lives. For example, linked spirals from the Mediterranean, interlace from the Celtic lands, Coyote and Thunderbird motifs from the Native Americans, and so on.

Talismans and amulets can be charged for varying lengths of time, depending upon the desired use. For simplicity and effectiveness, short-term amulets, as for safety or to obtain some goal, may be fashioned so that they can be renewed and reconsecrated by the individual twice a month. This would involve cleaning, censing (if possible), a lustral dipping, and a brief prayer to the Lady. The Priestess or Priest should set up proper methods and carefully inform those people receiving the charms and amulets of the proper care and recharging that will be necessary.

For complex tasks the creation of elemental beings is recommended.

Useful Herbs

Every Witch should learn as much as possible about the household, healing, and medicinal properties of herbs, and use them often. Sourcebooks such as the *Herbalist* and *Culpeper's Herbal* are recommended for study and use. The following are a few useful herbs which can be obtained from any herbal supply house or frequently near one's own home, and are good for starting your study.

Catnip: Mild stimulant much like Chinese tea. Serve it the same way.

Calendala: A teaspoon, freshly boiled in a cup of water, is a good antiseptic and healing balm.

Camomile Flowers: A mild sedative, serve as a tea. Brewed quite strong, Camomile is traditionally a "psychic condensing fluid" used for treating wands, Magic mirrors, etc.

Damiana Leaves: Mild aphrodisiac, served as a tea.

Eyebright: Filtered decoction of medium strength is an excellent eyewash. It can be used with camomile for psychic sensitizing of the eyes.

Garlic and Parsley: Mild stimulants; serve with other foods.

Horehound: Stimulant. Can be served as a tea; as a tonic it should be taken cold and three times the strength of the tea. For sore throat, gargle with double-strength tonic, take mixed with honey, or boil with sugar to make "cough drops."

Mugwort: Psychic sensitizer. Serve as a tea before scrying or Rites.

Nutmeg: For very loose bowels, take one-half teaspoon stirred into a cup of hot water, and steeped.

Peppermint Leaves: Stimulant, serve as a tea or use to flavor other foods.

Plantain Leaves: Antiseptic, stops bleeding very readily. Crush fresh young leaves and blot onto cuts.

NOTA BENE: The Herbalism books by Scott Cunningham are highly recommended as Herbal references. He used a format dealing with common usage, giving scientific and Old Religion names for most herbs.

Witch Prayers

The following prayers are useful as invocations before meals, prior to retiring at night, and in other cases where needed, and may be taught to children.

> *Bless us, O gracious Lady,*
> *And these thy gifts*
> *Which we have received of Thy bounty.*
> *Bless us, and draw us*
> *Ever closer to Thee.*
> *In Thy sacred Name … so be it.*
> (The Sign of the Pentagram may be made.)

Lady, though we can give nothing
That is not already yours,
Accept what we ourselves enjoy
As a token of our love,
In thanks for your care,
And in token of the giving of ourselves
To serve you.
Blessed Be!
(The Sign of the Pentagram may be made.)

Brigid, All-Mother,
Darling of the world,
Protector of children's beds,
Of maidens in love,
And of the rights of newlyweds,
Stay beside me and grant me thy favor.
Blessed Be!
(The Sign of the Pentagram may be made.)

Fair Goddess of the rainbow,
Of the stars and of the moon!
The Queen most powerful
Of Magic and the night!
I beg of thee thy aid,
That thou may'st give to me
Thy protection and thy love,
As I give mine to thee!
Blessed Be!
(The Sign of the Pentagram may be made.)

In preparing a child for bed it is meet and useful to have the small one perform a small ritual each evening under the guidance of a parent—to light a single candle, to say the prayer, and then to blow out the candle.

The Festivals of Witchcraft

The Rites of the festivals are contained in the Book of Shadows. The festivals should be held as close as possible to the times shown:

The Great Festivals, or Sabbats

Hallowe'en	(Samhain)	October 31
Lady Day	(Candlemas)	February 2
May Eve	(Beltane)	May 1
August Eve	(Lammas)	August 1

The Lesser Festivals or Sabbats

The Rite for Spring	First day of spring
Midsummer's Day	First day of summer
The Rite for Fall	First day of fall
Yule	First day of winter, or December 24–5

Esbats
    At each full moon

~

Signs, Colors, and Tarot Correspondences

Sign	Color	Tarot Card	Sign	Color	Tarot Card
Aries	red	Emperor	Libra	green	Justice
Taurus	red-orange	Hierophant	Scorpio	blue-green	Death
Gemini	orange	The Lovers	Sagittarius	blue	Temperance
Cancer	yellow-orange	Chariot	Capricorn	blue-violet	Devil
Leo	yellow	Strength	Aquarius	violet	Star
Virgo	yellow-green	Hermit	Pisces	red-violet	Moon

Tarot Suits and Cards Related to Elements

The Tarot suit of Wands and the Judgement card are assigned to the Fire element, Cups and the Hanged Man card to the Water element, Swords and the Fool card to the Air element, and Pentacles to the Earth element.

Music for Ritual Dances

A wide variety of music may be adapted for use in Craft Dancing, the only requirement being that it feel proper and appropriate to the coven members. In the past traditional music, such as English and European folk instrumental music, has been used to good effect. However, more modern types of music may be used.

New Age music is especially good since it has a very effective, other-worldly, exotic feel to it. Much of this music is long in duration, though some pieces of particular value are fairly short. It is useful, for any given ceremony, to record on tape an hour or more of the same music, so that the concentration of those in the circle may remain unbroken as long as necessary.

It is preferable to have one or more coven members within the circle actually playing instruments; the making of music is a form of Magic in itself. The table below shows some correlations with particular compositions.

PLANETARY CORRELATIONS

Planet	Metal	Tree	Incense	Music	Nerve Center	Tarot
Saturn	lead	alder F ⊤⊤⊤	myrrh	"Saturn"	sacral plexus	Universe
Jupiter	tin	oak D ⊥⊥	cedar	"Jupiter"	solar plexus	Wheel of Fortune
Mars	iron	holly T ⊥⊥⊥	ammonia	"Mars"	prostatic ganglion	Tower
Sun	gold	birch B ⊤	frankincense	"Hymn to the Sun"	cardiac plexus	The Sun
Venus	copper or brass	apple Q ⊥⊥⊥⊥⊥	rose	"Venus"	pharyngeal plexus	Empress
Mercury	quick-silver	hazel C ⊥⊥⊥⊥ ash N ⊤⊤⊤⊤⊤	storax	"Mercury"	pineal gland	Magician
Moon	silver	willow S ⊤⊤⊤⊤	jasmine	"Moonlight Sonata"	pituitary body	High Priestess
Earth			dittany			

"Hymn to the Sun" is by Handel, "Moonlight Sonata" by Beethoven; the rest are from "The Planets" suite by Holst.

The following compositions are frequently used, but many others could be chosen: "Rite of Spring," most of "The Planets," much of "Carmina Burana," the final movements of "Symphonie Fantastique," Ravel's "Bolero," de Falla's "Ritual Dance of Fire" (repeated several times), Walter Carlos' "Sonic Seasonings," and others. Also, modern neo-Pagan folk melodies can be very useful.

Training Time

It is normal within the Craft that a potential initiate should be trained and observed for the space of a year and a day. In the case of one who is unknown to the coven, or to any others that the coven may have good relations with, the year and the day should be adhered to for the safety of the coven. In the case of one who is known to the coven, or to others with whom the coven has good relations, or if the trainee has been referred by worthy acquaintances, this may be waived. Of course the trainee must have shown proficiency in all the subjects that a first level Initiate should know.

This proficiency should include the reading of most of the training material outlined in the "Grimoire of Shadows" and from the preferred reading list of the High Priestess.

Magical Alphabets

Every Witch will encounter times when an inscription will be needed for a spell on a Magical implement. Also, there may be times when some quiet or secret way of communication will be required which should go unnoticed by those not initiated.

There are a number of useful cipher alphabets which can be used, such as runes, hieroglyphics, the "angelic" script, Sanscrit, and others. Any of these may be studied, memorized, and used according to the Witch's own desire.

In the Craft the most common alphabets in use are the ancient Celtic Tree Alphabet, or Ogham, and various of the Norse or Anglo-Saxon runes. Great truths have been hidden for ages in the meanings behind the various letters and their ordering; for some hint of this the Witch should search in books on these subjects for in-depth lore.

Used merely as cipher alphabets, both Ogham and the Runes are best for inscribing Magical tools and very good for writing texts which must be protected. One's Craft name can be placed on a talisman, an inscription can be scribed on a Pentacle, or a few words (possibly disguised as a decoration on a card) can be left for oneself or for a friend. Every Witch should read extensively to discover the deeper meanings of both the Runes and Ogham.

Ogham, the Tree Alphabet

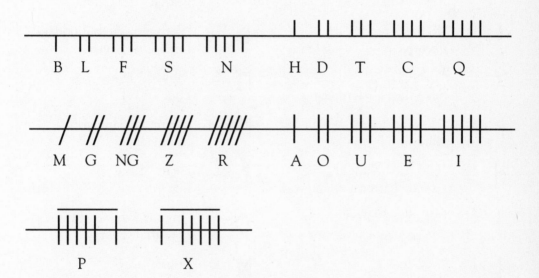

This Ogham system is based on the system used by Robert Graves in *The White Goddess*.

The Futhark Runes*

ᚠ	F	"Fehu," Prosperity Power		ᛇ	Y	Eihwaz, Yew Tree Axis, Life/Death
ᚢ	U	"Uruz," Auroch Manifestation		ᛈ	P	"Pertho," Dice Cup Karma
ᚦ	TH	"Thurisaz," Giant Destruction, Defense		ᛉ	Z	"Algiz," Protection Life
ᚨ	A	"Ansuz," God Reception, Transformation, Expression		ᛋ	S	"Sowilo," Sun Victory Rune
ᚱ	R	"Raidho," Wagon Right Action		ᛏ	T	"Tiawaz," the God Type Justice
ᚲ	K	"Kenaz," Torch Creativity		ᛒ	B	"Berhano, Birch Goddess Birth-Life-Death
ᚷ	G	"Gebo," G Sex, Magic, Sacrifice		ᛖ	E	"Ehwaz," Horse. Soul Travel
ᚹ	W	"Wunjo," Joy Harmony, Fellowship		ᛗ	M	"Mannaz," Human Intelligence
ᚺ	H	"Hagalaz," Hail, Egg Cosmic Pattern, Framework		ᛚ	L	Laguz," Lake Life
ᚾ	N	"Naudhiz " Head Persistence, Deliverance		ᛜ	NG	"Ingwaz," the God Ing Potential, Energy
ᛁ	I	"Isa," Ice World Ice, Concentration		ᛞ	D	Dagaz," Day Light
ᛃ	J	"Jera," Harvest Fertility, Peace		ᛟ	O	"Othla," Property Prosperity

The following symbols are added for greater ease in using runes.

ᛣ	C		∣ or ∼	J	ᚩ	O	ᚹ P
ᚠ	Q		ᚻ	Y	ᛨ	Z	

---

* This rune system is based on Icelandic and Danish sources. For a more comprehensive discussion of this rune system, see my book, *The Rites of Odin* (Llewellyn Publications, 1990).

Literature Relating to the Craft

There is a very considerable body of literature which pertains to the Craft, and which all should endeavor to read. The list below is not all-encompassing, but it is quite useful and can lead to other more specialized works: Where possible, publishers are indicated.

Witchcraft Today by Gerald Gardner
The Meaning of Witchcraft by Gerald Gardner
High Magick's Aid by Gerald Gardner
Witchcraft from the Inside by Raymond Buckland (Llewellyn Publications)
Witchcraft…The Religion by Raymond Buckland (Llewellyn Publications)
The Witches Speak by Patricia Crowther
Sign of the Labrys by Margaret St. Clair
The White Goddess by Robert Graves (Bantam Books)
The Golden Bough by Sir James Frazer
Aradia, Gospel of the Witches by Charles Leland
The Magick Arts in Celtic Britain by Spence
Gog and Magog by T. C. Lethbridge
Witches by T. C. Lethbridge
Watch the North Wind Rise by Robert Graves
A Step in the Dark by T. C. Lethbridge
The Divine King in England by Margaret Murray
God of the Witches by Margaret Murray (Doubleday)
The Witch Cult in Western Europe by Margaret Murray
Where Witchcraft Lives by Doreen Valiente
Any poetry by Robert Graves; he dedicates all of it to the Goddess.
Anything by Ray Buckland (Llewellyn Publications)
Anything by Scott Cunningham (Llewellyn Publications)
Anything by Doreen Valiente

The following do not deal with Witchcraft as such, but are particularly valuable:

The Secrets of Dr. Taverner by Dion Fortune
   (Aquarian Press or Samuel Weiser)
The Sea Priestess by Dion Fortune (Aquarian Press or Samuel Weiser)
Moon Magic by Dion Fortune (Aquarian Press or Samuel Weiser)
The Demon Lover by Dion Fortune (Aquarian Press)

Psychic Self Defense by Dion Fortune (Aquarian Press)
Applied Magic by Dion Fortune (Aquarian Press or Samuel Weiser)
Aspects of Occultism by Dion Fortune (Aquarian Press)
Initiation into Hermetics by Franz Bardon
    (Osiris-Verlag. Kettig Über Koblenz, Germany)
The Practice of Magical Evocation by Franz Bardon
    (Osiris-Verlag. Kettig Über Koblenz, Germany)
The Key to the Tarot by Lauron W. DeLaurence
The Herbalist by J. E. Meyer
Magical Ritual Methods by William Gray (Aquarian Press)
Growing the Tree Within by William Gray (Llewellyn Publications)

There are many more good books. Check with your Priestess or Priest for a more up-to-date listing.

~

PART II

MAGICAL THEORY

Magical Theory

In the study and practice of Magic, it is important that you adopt the proper mental attitude: the feeling that anything can be accomplished if one desires and wills that it be done. In other words, you may bring forth anything that you resolve to bring forth!

In studying Magic you should, for a while, set aside the critical, "that can't happen because ..." attitude which has been ingrained in all of us by our current technological society. For the time being, accept that Magic and its various principles are what they claim to be, and in time you will see that the Ancient Arts do not contradict science, but supplement it by filling in an area that science does not yet cover.

Magic is as logically structured as modern physics, and can give reproductive results in exactly the same way, but it also requires a similar amount of study and training in order to get results.

Science and Magic overlap in one noteworthy area, the field of psychology, where facets common to both may be found. You may find that reading works on psychology, particularly the works of Dr. Karl Jung, will aid your Magical studies.

The Elements

In Magic one uses the four elements of earth, air, fire, and water, plus the fifth element called akasha, or the "life force." Except in rare cases, these do not appear in pure form on the physical plane, but they are very much in evidence in the astral and mental planes. The traditional signs, colors, etc. are listed below.

Color	Symbol	Element	Tarot Relationship
White	◯	Akasha	————————
Bright Red	△ (with bar)	Fire	Suit of Swords
Yellow	△	Air	The Suit of Wands
Blue	▽	Water	The Suit of Cups
Green	▽ (with bar)	Earth	Suit of Pentacles

THE PRINCIPLE OF FIRE

The basic qualities we associate with the fire element are heat and expansion.

Every element has two "polarities" or two ways in which it may act. For example, when the fire element is in its active or positive mode, it is constructive and creative. When it is in its passive or negative mode it is destructive and dissecting.

There is a certain Magical force which is very closely related to the fire element and which is similar to electricity in many ways. For want of a better term, we will call it the "electrical fluid," and note that it relates to the expansion of the fire element. Uses for this force will be explained later.

THE PRINCIPLE OF WATER

The basic qualities we associate with the water element are coldness and shrinkage.

When the water element is in its active or positive mode, it is life-giving, nourishing and protective. In its passive or negative mode, it is dissecting, fermenting and dividing.

There is another Magical force which is very closely related to the water element, and similar in magnetism in many ways. For want of a better word, we will call it "magnetic fluid," and note that it relates to the shrinking and contraction of the water element. Uses for this force will be discussed later.

THE PRINCIPLE OF AIR

The air element is related to both fire and water, and in fact is the "mediator" or balance between the active and the passive activities of fire and water.

The air element has the dryness of fire and the humidity of water.

THE PRINCIPLE OF EARTH

The earth element is related to air, fire, and water, and in fact involves all of the other three in a solid form.

The properties of the earth element are heaviness, solidity, and closeness.

Since the earth element combines fire and water, as well as air, we may consider the fluid in its vicinity as "electromagnetic." This force has uses we will discuss later.

THE PRINCIPLE OF AKASHA

The akasha or "ether," often called the "life force," is the basic substance of the universe, and all the other elements are derived from it. Akasha pervades all things, yet it is also "the Cause" of all which exists. The etheric principle bypasses time and space, and is to a great degree beyond our understanding, though with proper training a Witch may use it to advantage in Magic.

KARMA — THE LAW OF CAUSE AND EFFECT

The law of cause and effect is rooted in the akasha principle, and thus is not affected by time or space. This immutable law works everywhere in the most obvious to the most extremely subtle manner.

Every deed of ours either proceeds from a cause or is followed by a result, whether in the blinking of an eye or in two thousand years. An ancient saying of the Craft is "the good you do, shall be returned to thee ... three times over." This is derived from Karma.

The balancing-out of cause and effect may take place from moment to moment, day to day, year to year, or over a number of your incarnations. The significance of karma is very deep indeed, a subject that deserves thought and additional study.

Humanity

The human being is the universe in miniature, physically speaking. He or she is influenced by the cosmos, and can in turn influence the cosmos.

Disharmony in the body manifests itself in sickness, while harmony manifests itself in strength, health, and beauty. The functioning of the four elements in their proper aspects is *most* important in keeping the body in its best condition.

According to the most ancient tradition, the body has four basic divisions; the feet, the legs, and the bowels relating to the earth element; the abdomen relating to the water element; the chest relating to the air element; the shoulders, the neck, and the head relating to the fire element. These divisions are of great importance in Magic.

Your body itself is the prime tool used in Magic, as various combinations of elements or electrical and magnetic fluids can be concentrated intensely within your physical and astral frame while you set up a Magical operation or "spell." As you project this accumulated power outward and away with a sword, wand, or pentacle, the Magical instruments merely serve as channels and a means of direction for the Magic within yourself.

The body has its natural polarities, and Magic should work through these. For a right-handed person the right side of the body is active and electrical, while the left side is passive and magnetic.

All the elemental principles should be in balance within the body, each operating in both its positive (constructive) and negative (destructive) modes. For example, if your body possesses excessive fire element you will be thirsty, excessive air element will result in hunger, excessive water element will make one cold, and excessive earth element will make you tired.

Manipulation of the elements and the electromagnetic fluids within the body can lead to some very striking results in your Magical operations. This too will be covered in later sections, as much training of the body and mind is required.

THE ELEMENTS IN THE MATERIAL WORLD

Just as the human body must operate with a balance of the elements, so also must the world we live in depend upon a balance of elemental forces and electromagnetic fluids. In the section above we saw how the elements could affect the body; now pause for a moment and draw an analogy between the body and the world, and you will see that all the everyday happenings about us can be caused by interactions of the elements.

As an exercise, try figuring out everyday happenings and reactions over the space of one day by using the four-element system.

The Mind and the Astral Body

The mind, the personality, and the astral body are all intimately tied into the four elements and the akasha. An electromagnetic fluid connects the body and the soul, and extends about your body for two or three feet in every direction.

The elements control the personality, and a shortage or excess of any element is manifested in the personality features (and thus also the character) of a person. A few examples of elemental influences on temperament are given on the next page. Many more could be added to these lists.

Choleric (Fire)
Active
		Passive	
activity	enthusiasm	gluttony	jealousy
eagerness	resolution	passion	irritability
courage	productivity	intemperance	destructiveness

Sanguine (Air)
Active
		Passive	
diligence	adroitness	contempt	gossiping
kindness	clearness	slyness	lack of endurance
optimism	lack of grief	dishonesty	garrulity
cheerfulness	independence	fickleness	
joy	familiarity	continual feeling of being affronted	
capacity for penetrating			

Melancholic (Water)
Active
		Passive	
devotion	respectability	apathy	indifference
modesty	compassion	shyness	depression
docility	seriousness	laziness	
fervor	cordiality		
calmness	comprehension		
confiding	meditation		
forgiveness	tenderness		

Phlegmatic (Earth)
Active
		Passive	
reputation	respectability	insipidity	unscrupulousness
endurance	consideration	dullness	misanthropy
resolution	firmness	tardiness	unreliability
sobriety	seriousness	laconism	
objectivity	scrupulousness		
resistance	thoroughness		
punctuality	reservedness		
confidence	responsibility		
circumspection			

∼

The Aura

All of the influences within one's temperament show in the *aura*, which exhibits a certain characteristic color. The aura itself results from the active and passive actions of the elements within the body. By seeing the color of the aura, you can tell quite accurately what a person's character is. Seeing or sensing the aura will be covered later.

The astral body has two centers within the brain: the cerebrum, the seat of normal consciousness, and the cerebellum, the seat of the subconscious.

The astral body possesses "psychic centers" which generally match the major centers in the physical body and which seem to form definite links between the physical and the astral. In the physically undeveloped or psychically dormant individual these centers are not active. By training or by religious experience the psychic centers may be opened properly and the natural, Magical forces of the world about us may be drawn through the centers and put to good use. Drugs and shattering emotional crises may also open the psychic centers, but in these cases, the opening is sudden and the results are usually disastrous, as the unfortunate individual normally has no idea of how to control the powerful forces which have begun flooding through his or her astral body.

The proper opening of the psychic centers is an important facet of Hindu and Tibetan Magic (and others), and one with which you should familiarize yourself through further reading. The training you will receive in the Outer Court will begin the opening of these centers within yourself, but it will be a gradual process of training and practice.

Indian philosophy calls the psychic centers "lotuses" and the awakening of these lotuses are called "Kundalini Yoga." The centers are:

Muladhara — earthy; lowest part of the soul

Swadhistana — water; the sexual organs

Manipura — the center of the soul; the umbilical region; fire

Anahata — compensatory, the heart; air

Visudha — the neck; akasha

Anja — volition and intellect; located between the eyebrows

Sahasrara — the highest and most divine of the centers, the "thousand leafed lotus"; near the pineal gland; all other psychic centers are controlled by this

Susumna — akasha; located with the spine and links all the psychic centers

The psychic centers are known by various names in Western traditions, and the ascribed locations may vary slightly, but generally they are close to the same.

The Astral Plane

The astral plane is not created of the four elements, but is rather a manifestation of the akasha principle. Hence, everything in the material world which has happened, is happening, and will happen has its origin, regulation, and existence in the astral. Since akasha is the original source of all things and since it is timeless, you can, with training and practice, travel to any time or place via the astral.

The astral plane, in addition to extending beyond time and space, has various kinds of inhabitants. Those who have died on the earth plane are here, in what we would call the "Summer Land." Larvae, or beings which have consciously or unconsciously been brought into life on the astral plane by intense emotional thinking, are present. These are a low order of intelligence, but possess a strong sense of self preservation. Consciously created elemental beings also exist on the astral plane; these can be of high intelligence and of considerable aid to one who uses Magic, and instructions for their creation are given in a later section. Beings of the four pure elements are to be found in the astral: salamanders in the element of fire, sylphides or gremlins of the air element, mermaids or undines of the water element, and gnomes of the earth element. There are a host of other beings who are spoken of in ancient legends, and who seem to have been related to us in the past: satyrs, wood maidens, watergoblins, centaurs, and wood sprites, for instance.

The inhabitants of the astral plane seldom seem to encounter other types of inhabitants: elemental beings, for example, are of a much higher vibration than larvae, and different yet from the undines, so that each is completely separated from the others. With development of clairvoyance it is possible to see and contact all who live on the astral.

The Spirit

The body and the soul serve only as a veil or garment for the spirit. The spirit is the immortal part and created in the image of the Ancient Ones. It is not easy to define something divine, immortal and imperishable, yet put into correct terms with all else, yet a few words can be said on the subject, and the rest left to meditation.

The spirit has its source in the akasha. Its primary elemental principles are:

Will (volition) — Fire — Strength, Power, Passion

Intellect (mind) — Air — Memory, Judgment, Discrimination

Life and feeling — Water — Conscience, Intuition

Ego — Earth — Egotism, Confidence, Self-Preservation

Faith — Akasha

The Mental Plane

As the body has its earthly plane, and the astral body or soul owns the astral plane, so also does the mind have its own sphere: the mental plane. Like the other planes, it originates in the akasha.

Just as the astral body, through the electromagnetic fluid of the astral world, forms an "astral matrix" about the physical body, so also does the electromagnetic fluid of the mental world form a "mental matrix" linking the mental body to the astral body.

Ideas and thoughts have their origin in the akasha, and enter the material world by way of the mental body.

The mental sphere is bound to neither time nor space.

Like the astral, the mental plane is inhabited. "Ideal forms" exist here, and also the deceased whose astral bodies have been dissolved by the elements in maturity towards perfection. Here also are the elemental beings which are created by conscious thought of the human mind. Absolute perfection is possible here, as explained by the ancient Greek philosophers Socrates and Plato.

God Force

In the Craft we know of the Old Ones and count them as our friends, yet we realize that beyond them are yet others who are greater. As Witches and human beings it normally suffices that we know the Lady, the God, and then the Old Ones, but for Magical purposes what is the nature of the "god forces"?

The Ultimate is inconceivable, intangible, and incomprehensible, yet we are a part of it. Through the practice of Magic we tap some small bit of this force and gradually gain an understanding which is far beyond that of our fellow men.

The god-force can be approached from the four elements:

Fire — Almightiness and Omnipotence

Air — Wisdom, Purity, and Clearness (thus, Universal Lawfulness)

Water — Love and Eternal Life

Earth — Omnipresence and Immortality (thus, Eternity)

There is much more to Magical theory, of course, and much further reading is recommended, specifically the works of Franz Bardon and William E. Butler, but the above is sufficient for the Magical training and practice in this grimoire.

Consider and meditate upon what has been said.

PART III

THE MAGICAL ARTS

Magic Circles

THE TRIPLE CIRCLE

The Magic Circle is the most important device used in the practice of Magic. According to tradition, when a Circle is cast those within will "travel between the worlds." To a Witch, the Circle is at the very edge of several dimensions at once during a rite; odd and unusual things will happen within and about the ritual circle during a ceremony. Indeed, psychically sensitive people will often sense almost continuous "happenings" in the area.

Those who are in a circle are at a "zero point" of time, space, and events—hence the tradition of the three circles.

The circle is to be used not only for Magic, but as a safeguard for the mind, to keep Magical and psychic phenomena—and the mind itself—firmly under control. Thus, when the Triple Circle is used, the images of the subconscious and of the psychic will manifest themselves only within and about the circle, and will not intrude on a Witch's everyday life on their own accord.

When a Witch performs even daily psychic exercises, she or he should draw a Triple Circle about her- or himself, if only in the Witch's imagination. This not only protects the mind but serves to put one apart from the world. In evocation of elementals, whether natural or created, the Magical circle should always be employed, even if such an evocation is "merely" done as an exercise of the imagination.

THE MAGIC TRIANGLE

The Magical Triangle is only rarely used by Witches, being more a device of ceremonial Magic; still, it is at times used for visualization and materialization exercises. For example, it may be quite useful to put a crystal ball or a Magic mirror inside a Magic Triangle to increase its effectiveness.

The Magic Triangle shall be used at times when a Witch desires the manifestation of an elemental or artificial being within certain bounds, but not necessarily in the same circle with the Witch herself. The triangle should be about five feet on a side, although it can be larger or smaller if desired, and should have one angle pointing directly at the Witch's ritual circle a few feet away.

The triangle may be sketched, painted, or merely consecrated in the imagination. Materialization will be aided in a rite if a candle is placed at each apex of the triangle and a Magic mirror is set within the triangle, facing toward the Triple Circle.

It must be said again, that the Magic Triangle is seldom used by Witches.

THE GREAT AND SMALL CIRCLES

The Great Circle is the gathering place of Witches to celebrate the festivals and to work Magic as a coven. The rites are as listed in the various Books of Shadows and usually do not vary much. The Great Circle is, by Tradition, nine feet across, although for certain rites it is prescribed to be fifteen feet across.

A man and a woman, or two or three people who do not include a Priestess among their number, may set up a Small Circle for the practice of Magic. The Small Circles and the Magic performed therein may vary greatly, depending upon the goals and the desires of the individual Witches. If two Witches desire to "travel between the worlds" to meditate or to contact spirits or elemental beings, or to weave a spell, the Small Circle may be cast with such ceremony as seems appropriate. Some of the training in the Grimoire of the Shadows may require the use of a Small Circle.

MAGIC AND CEREMONIES OUTDOORS

Witchcraft is, by its very nature, a religion of the open air, of forests and mountains, of clear, starry skies and firelight. The Magic of the Craft will always work better in places such as these, but in the present day world these things are seldom attainable for the performance of our Rites, and we must usually be content to work Magic and commune with the Old Ones in a curtained room or within the cellar of a house.

Still, each coven should try, whenever possible, to have Rites outdoors in some wild and remote area. This might be only once a year, but it would be very rewarding.

Small Circles, being often far less formal, may frequently be held by two or more individuals in a grove of trees, along a beach, or any place where there is some privacy.

NOTE BENE: The work of training in *A Grimoire of Shadows* is a very individual sort of Magic and can often be done while walking across fields or through wooded areas. It is strongly recommended that as much of this training as possible be accomplished in the open air for stronger Magic and faster development.

STONE CIRCLES AND HENGES

Stone circles and henges are great conductors and storage facilities for Magical power. Magic worked in a henge is particularly powerful, and the experience of doing such Magic is magnificent!

Witches who have their own homes or lands often build stone circles or henges in some remote part of their property. It is recommended.

The Pentagram

The Pentagram has been used since long before the dawn of history as a salutation to the Goddess in her Astarte-aspect, as Empress of the Sea, and was once customarily tattooed on a sailor's Mound of Venus between the thumb and forefinger of his right hand. This practice is occasionally seen today, though the original meaning has been lost to the men of the sea.

In ancient Greece it was worn in the same manner by initiates of the Mysteries. The lengths of the various lines in the pentagram gave the basic pitch and tone of all music, and also gave the basic ideal lengths and proportions of all classical architecture. It also related to the size and shape of the world (which was known accurately in those days) and gave insights into other worlds and the universe beyond.

The pentagram has always represented the concept of "humankind made perfect," incorporating the concepts of all the elements (earth, air, fire, water, and life) in balance within the body and soul of the highest beings that the human race has to offer. Further, the flow of the entire universe requires a harmony in these elements, from the most cosmic macrocosm to the most tiny microcosm.

The pentagram also gives the various paths to the understanding of High Magic, though this and more profound meanings—and the advanced uses of this sign—are best learned in the Mystery Schools and the Elders training of the best Witchcraft covens. Even so, it is strongly recommended that the Witch make an especially intensive research into traditions related to the Pentagram, and do much meditation upon its symbolism.

Displaying the Pentagram between the fingers of Aphrodite and Zeus showed the relation of humankind, science, art, and Magic to the Gods. It also indicated from whence came the inspiration and Power for all of these high arts, and of all living beings.

When in use, this sign may also be known as the Pentacle.

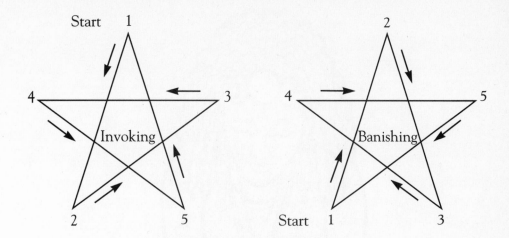

INVOKING AND BANISHING PENTAGRAMS

The Sign of the Pentagram is the ancient sign of salutation to the Goddess, the God, and to the High Forces. Also, the pentagrams are drawn during the calling and dismissal of Forces during the ceremonies, and in greeting and bidding farewell to the Gods.

The pentagram is drawn in the air with the athame or sword, and occasionally the wand or the first two fingers of the right hand, with the Witch seeing it in his or her mind as a star of glowing blue fire being scribed in the air, and sent forth into the realms of Magic with the final salute by a thrust through its center-point after kissing the blade or wand.

The banishing pentagram is of value as a simple form of protection when drawn in the air to banish any evil or negative influences that the individual Witch may regard as threatening.

THE SIGN OF THE PENTACLE

As a sign of salutation to the Great Ones during the Rites, or as a personal sign of devotion to the Goddess (or God) when one is alone, it is proper to make the sign of the Pentacle.

The fingers of Fire and Wisdom of the right hand shall be touched lightly to the center of the forehead, right breast, left shoulder, right shoulder, left breast, and forehead in turn. You may draw a pentacle in the air before you as a sign of blessing.

A related and extremely ancient tradition of the Craft is to kiss the right hand to the Moon when first you see Her at night. This is a salute and gesture of devotion to the Lady.

Magical Accessories and Clothing for Wearing within the Circle

MAGICAL JEWELRY

Every female Witch shall wear a beaded necklace when within the ritual circle or when involved in Magical work. This necklace symbolizes the many lives through which we must pass to achieve perfection.

Other jewelry may be worn by men and women and is recommended, since rings, earrings, pendants, bracelets, and other jewelry will absorb considerable power during Magical operations and soon will be Magical tools, which can serve well in a Witch's everyday life.

MAGICAL GARMENTS

The Inner Court of Witchcraft often performs its rites with the Initiates being "sky-clad." In the Outer Court there is a lesser amount of Magical experience, and to maintain the proper control the members must therefore wear robes. Only in the rare cases when High Magic is needed will the Priestess authorize sky-clad ritual.

Long robes of suitable design shall be worn by all Witches. The robes may have hoods and long sleeves, but this is by no means mandatory. Silk or silk-like material is recommended but not required. The color may be as chosen by each individual Witch. Ideally, the individual should have made his or her own robe. If the Witch lacks the necessary skills, she or he must, however, have done some sewing, repair, or made some personal addition to his or her robe: it must reflect the individual. Each Witch must also wash and iron his or her own robe; the mark of the owner must be everywhere upon it.

Except in the coldest weather, neither shoes nor underclothes will be worn.

If one wishes to choose colors which are in consonance with astrological principles, the following can be used in selecting robes:

Saturn — Dark Violet   **Venus** — Green

Jupiter — Blue   **Mercury** — Opalescent

Mars — Purple   **Moon** — Silver or White

Sun — Yellow, Gold, or Orange

The Magical Belt

The Magical belt, cord, or girdle is put around the waist to hold the robe together and in place. On occasions when a baldric is worn, it also is held in place by having the belt or sash fastened over it. This symbolism is deep, for the cord or girdle fastened or tied about the waist forms a circle around the body, signifying that the Witch is the Cosmos in miniature and masters the elements by living and working in consonance with nature.

If a cord is worn, the loose ends when tied should hang down to the knees or below. The Magical belt or girdle may be as wide as a cummerbund, or it may be a narrower belt of leather. Except for certain rites it must be red, for red is the ancient color of life, and the sacred life-blood. It now also symbolizes the blood of the millions of martyrs who died for the Craft in the terrible Time of the Burnings.

The Circlet, Magus-Band, or Horned Helmet

When carrying out Magical operations, the badge of the Priestess or Priest shall be a circlet, headband, or helmet. This, like the belt, is a symbol of the perfection of the intellect and emotion, of power over things great and small—the crowning expression of Magical power.

The headgear should only be put on the Witch's head when she or he is fully absorbed with the thought of being one with the Goddess or God. When the circlet, magus-band, or helmet is fitted to the head, the atmosphere must immediately become that of a temple or ritual circle.

The headgear may, like the belt, be decorated with the symbols showing the Witch's oneness with, and mastery of, the elements.

Bracelets and Rings, Anklets and Foot Jewelry

It is well to wear jewelry within the circle, for such items will soon become psychically charged and useful talismans for such purposes as the Witch does desire. The Priestess and the Priest especially should wear bracelets of silver engraved with their respective Craft names, and pentacles or crescents. Any lettering should of course be done in the Tree alphabet or one of the other Magical scripts.

Rings of sentimental importance, preferably of silver and ideally with one or more mounted jewels, should be worn as a Magical link with the Old Ones.

The wearing of foot-jewelry and anklets, of traditional or modern design, adds subtly in the performance of Magical rituals. Men may wear leathern straps in the ancient style, and women may choose whatever material or style they so desire.

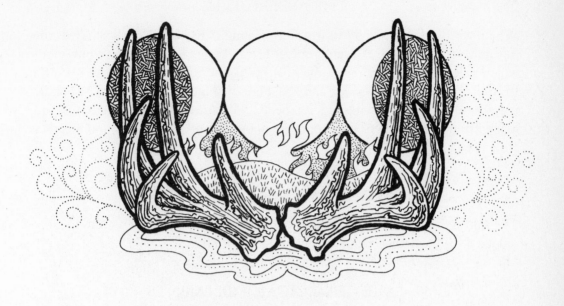

Magical Equipment

GODDESS AND GOD IMAGES

The Goddess and God images are to be symbolic of the two deities of Witchcraft. The Goddess shall always be represented as a beautiful woman, skyclad. The God is to be represented as a powerfully built, horned man, he is also skyclad. According to very ancient tradition, the Horned God can also be represented by a bull's head or a set of bull's horns, either full size or in miniature.

NOTA BENE: God statues are little used these days, as many Witches prefer to use antlers. Usually the antlers are placed behind, around, or to either side of the Goddess statue.

THE INCENSE BRAZIER

The incense brazier or thurible should be metal, of rugged construction, and provided with a handle or a chain for use when hot. A lid is useful for keeping the sparks confined. It is best to use glowing charcoal blocks in the brazier, set atop clean sand, and to sprinkle in powdered incense one or two teaspoonsfull at a time.

THE ASPERGILLIS

Whenever the Rites specify that water or wine is to be ritually sprinkled, the aspergillis is to be used. A useful aspergillis can be made by cutting a one-inch-wide circle, ball, or star from a piece of sponge and tacking it to the end of a wooden handle five inches long and about one-half inch in diameter. The handle may then be carved as desired, sanded, and painted black. Alternately, an aspergillis may be made of sprigs of mint, marjoram, or rosemary, bound together with a red silken thread.

SALT AND WATER CONTAINERS

The salt and water for consecration may be put into small open containers of unique design, whether metal or ceramic.

CARE OF MAGICAL IMPLEMENTS

All items used ritually should not be used for mundane purposes. They should instead be cleaned after use, wrapped in silk or silk-like material, and stored away until the next Rite. Sword, Cup, Wand, and Pentacle may be displayed if so desired, but in such a location that they cannot be casually touched. One's own athame is a very personal implement and should be handled only by oneself, so that the Magical charge on it will not be weakened.

CONSECRATION OF TOOLS

Instruments for use within the Great and Small Circles, as well as amulets, talismans, and other items shall be consecrated by performing the Simple Rite of Magic, with Consecration before the Goddess as the goal. The length of time for the loading, a year, three years, thirteen years, a lifetime or longer, must be set before the Rite. Tools to be consecrated are the athames, wands, swords, cups, pentacles, incense braziers, Goddess images, God images, bracelets, anklets, and other jewelry.

ALTAR TOOLS

Athame

Each Witch shall have an athame, or sacred, black-handled knife. This is the basic, traditional, and most powerful of tools. It should be consecrated at the time a Witch is initiated and should be used by no other person. The athame should never be used for cutting, and should never draw blood. The athame is strong protection at any time and gains strength as it is used . . . no force of darkness can stand before it. The athame is double edged; a Witch shall inscribe on the handle only a pentagram and her Witch-name in runes.

Sword

The sword has the power of the athame, but is normally used only for rituals. Any double-bladed sword may be consecrated and used; preferably it should be old. A simple exorcism or psychic cleansing should be performed before consecration, and a Pentacle inscribed on the pommel and on each side of the blade near the hilt. Traditionally, the sword, like the athame, governs the element of air.

Wand

The wand should be twelve to eighteen inches in length and may be slender or as much as an inch thick. It should be cut from a living willow tree (after asking the

tree's permission and explaining the reason), and soaked or left with the leaves and allowed to live for three days in Simple Condenser, (strong camomile tea), then peeled, dried, and polished black. If desired, it may be tipped in silver. According to tradition, it governs the fire element.

Cup

Any large and preferably silver cup or goblet may be consecrated and used. According to tradition, it governs the water element.

Pentacle

The pentacle should be seven to eight inches in diameter, circular, and made of either wood or metal. One side may be painted flat white, the other, dull black. Inscribe the figure on the white side (the black side may be used as a mirror). According to tradition, the pentacle governs the earth element.

NOTA BENE: For more information on Magical tools, their use, and training with them, see Part VII.

SUBSTITUTIONS IN MAGICAL EQUIPMENT

The "Outer Court Book of Shadows" makes many specifications concerning altar design, design and treating of the wand, pentacle, sword, amulets, lamps, robes, and so forth. Not all Witches, it is realized, will have the necessary skills or the resources to prepare everything as specified. Therefore, substitutions may be made: any low table could be used instead of a black and white altar; if calendala herb is not available; the wand and Magical condensing powder may be made without it; if no sword is in the Witches' possession an athame may be used in the Rites, and so on.

In the Craft there is one overall rule which applies as law, in ritual, and in equipage: it is not the form which is important; that which ultimately counts the most is the intent behind it.

Above all, the Witch's own hands, eyes, and mind are all the equipage that is really necessary!

THE UNIVERSAL CONDENSER

Take two level teaspoons each of camomile and eyebright and put into a bowl. Bring two cups of water to a boil and pour it over the herbs. Cover immediately. Allow to steep and cool for fifteen minutes.

Filter the tea through four layers of purified linen. The filtered liquid is a Universal Condenser, a fluid that can be used medicinally as a lotion, Magically for a ritual, or to improve clairvoyance. Diluted with seven parts warm water, it is good for a stomach ache, and it is slightly laxative. Straight it can be used for aches and pains by applying it with cotton every two hours. To improve clairvoyance, put pads soaked in the elixir on the eyes, leaving them there twenty to twenty-five minutes.

Localized sensitivity (occult) can be induced by applying the liquid to part concerned. (i.e., the palms of the hands or the soles of the feet.)

INCENSE

The use of incense makes the vicinity of the circle a place even more congenial to the Old Ones, and aids the power of the rituals in transporting the circle and those in it to be "between the worlds." Sandalwood is frequently used in Witch rites, although this is by no means a fixed choice. Powdered incense is the most useful form; it is sprinkled on glowing charcoal blocks. In ritual Magic a different category of incense is used when dealing with each of the planetary influences, but such detail is unnecessary in the craft.

PREPARATION OF A MAGIC MIRROR

In the Outer Court of Witchcraft, the mirror plays a major role as the portal or window to other worlds, a means of communicating with even the most exalted entities, a means for ordinary divination, a storage for psychic energy, etc. Such a mirror can be of any size or shape, although larger ones are easier to use. In all cases, the mirror back must be not silvered but black.

The ideal Magical mirror should be concave, as the odd optical effects tend to heighten the user's sensitivity. The best mirror would be made from an old-fashioned oval picture frame and curved glass, treated as below. However, the curved glass from an old wall clock, the curved reflecting glass from the front of an old video set, or the slightly concave glass sold to be the rear window on certain types of old automobiles are satisfactory so long as some sort of wooden frame may be fitted to the finished mirror.

To begin, the glass and the wooden frame must be thoroughly cleansed. If the frame is scarred it should be sanded and repainted. The glass should be rinsed for three minutes (carefully) in running water which is cold or at least cool. While rinsing, fix firmly in your mind that the water is carrying away all base influences which have ever been near the glass . . . that psychically as well as physically, the glass is perfectly clean. Set the glass on a clean, freshly washed white cloth, and let it dry in the air.

When dry, the glass may be moved to sheets of clean paper for painting. Black paint from a freshly opened can should be used. The back of the mirror, i.e., the convex side, is the side that should be painted. Use as many coats as necessary to completely blacken the mirror such that no light at all can come through it.

When the last coat has dried, the mirror may again be placed on the clean cloth for the final consecration. Prepare some Magical condensing fluid—some very strong camomile tea is appropriate—and place your hands over the fluid in an attitude of blessing, saying the following and picturing it in your mind:

> **Now do I breathe of the pure white light**
> **Which pervades the universe.**
> **And as I breathe out the light goes forth**
> **From my hands into the potion before me,**
> **Where it shall always remain.**
> **Into this shall all forces be drawn**
> **In the Name of our Gracious Goddess.**
> (Sign of Pentacle)

With a clean, new brush, paint the condensing fluid directly onto the painted surface, or onto a clean, new blotter to be fitted against the glass. Place your hands over it in an attitude of Blessing, saying:

> **In the Name of the Lady**
> **May only good and high influences**
> **Come through this Mirror.**
> **So Be It!**
> (Sign of Pentacle)

After drying, seal the back of the Magic Mirror permanently against dust. Begin using the mirror ritually as soon as possible.

PART IV

RITUALS OF PASSAGE

Magical Names

Shortly after being initiated into the First Level, a Witch should choose and take a Magical name, or "Craft Name." Such a name is usually drawn from Celtic or British legend or history, although Norse, ancient Germanic, or Gaulish are sometimes used. These names are almost always the only ones used in ritual or Magic, especially within the Great Circle.

The name chosen should, most importantly, be one which "feels most comfortable" to the individual. It is the name which will appear on talismans for a Witch's use, and the one by which he or she will best be known to fellow Craft members.

~

The Naming Ritual

When a Witch has decided upon a Craft name, he or she will notify the Priestess and Priest and arrange to be named at the next Great Circle. (Consecrated water must be available.) The Naming Ritual shall take place after the Great Circle has been cast. If the Witch be a man, he shall be named by the Priestess, if the Witch be a woman, she shall be named by the Priest.

The Priestess/Priest shall call on the one to be named to kneel before the altar, facing north. The Priestess/Priest shall walk to the north of the altar and, taking up the sword or the athame in hand, ask:

> **O thou of the ancient Craft**
> **By what Magical name**
> **Dost thou desire to be known**
> **Before our Gracious Lady**
> **And Her powerful Consort?**

The kneeling Witch will say the new name, and the Priestess/Priest shall with the sword (or athame) touch the kneeling one on the left shoulder, right shoulder, and the top of the head, saying:

With this name shalt thou be known in the Circle,
With this name shalt thou work
The Magic of the forests,
With this name shalt thou be sanctified.
I do name thee_____.

The Priest/Priestess shall then replace the sword (or athame) and walk sunwards around the altar to the kneeling Witch and, raising him/her to a standing position, face the east and walk to the eastern point of the circle. The Priestess/Priest, standing just behind the one to be named, shall spread both arms outward and proclaim:

O thou beings of the air
See and know the Witch_____.
Hearken unto his/her chants,
As thou wouldst serve the Goddess.

They both make the Sign of the Pentacle. This proclamation is repeated for fire at the south, water at the west, and earth at the north, making the sign of the Pentacle each time. Then they perform a final, quiet pentacle at the east.

The Priestess/Priest then stands before the altar with the Witch being named and takes in hand the vessel of the consecrated water. The first two fingers of the right hand are dipped into the water and touched to the left breast, dipped in the water and touched to the forehead, dipped into the water and touched to the right breast, and so on to make the Sign of the Pentacle. The Priestess/Priest says:

By the name of_____
Shalt thou have power and knowledge
Of earth, of air, of fire, of water,
Of the force of Life itself
In the service of the Goddess.

As they face to the north, the Priestess/Priest replaces the vessel of consecrated water and picks up the sword (or athame) and, holding it out to the north, says:

O thou Gracious and lovely Goddess of the wilds,
O thou God who art protector and bringer of joy,
See before thee the Witch_____,
    thy friend and servant.

**Help him/her along the Way, to know the richness
   of Life.
So be it!**

The Priestess/Priest salutes, and the Witch who has been named makes the sign of the Pentacle, and is embraced by the Priestess/Priest.

They sit and wine is poured for all the coven. A toast is made:

**To our good friend
The Witch_____
And to the Old Ones!**

NOTA BENE: Other rituals or workings of Magic should be done at this time to enable the Witch to use her/his new name.

~

The Self-Blessing Ritual

This ritual should be performed during the new moon, but it is not limited to that phase. Need, not season, determines the performance. There is real power in the self-blessing; it should be used in time of need and not promiscuously.

The purpose of the rite is to bring the individual into closer contact with the Godhead. It can also be used as a minor dedication, when a person who desires dedication has no Witch, whether Priestess, Priest, or coven member, to perform such a ritual. The Self-Blessing Rite may be used as a minor exorcism, to banish any evil influences which may have formed about the person. It may be performed by any person upon her/himself, at their desire.

Perform the rite in a quiet place, free of distractions, and nude. You will need the following:

1. Salt, about one-quarter teaspoon

2. Wine, about an ounce

3. Water, about one-half ounce

4. Candle, votive or other

The result of the Rite is a feeling of peace and calm.

When you are ready to begin, sprinkle the salt on the floor and stand on it, lighting the candle. Let the warmth of the candle be absorbed into your body. Mix the water into the wine, meditating upon your reasons for performing the self blessing.

Read the following aloud:

Bless me, Mother for I am Thy child.

Dip the fingers of the right hand into the mixed water and wine and anoint the eyes:

Blessed Be my eyes, that I may see Thy path.

Anoint the nose:

Blessed Be my nose, that I may breathe Thy essence.

Anoint the mouth:

Blessed Be my mouth, that I may speak of Thee.

Anoint the breast:

Blessed Be my breast, that I may be faithful in my works.

Anoint the loins:

Blessed Be my loins, which bring forth the life of humanity as Thou hast brought forth all creation.

Anoint the feet:

Blessed Be my feet, that I may walk in Thy ways.

It is very desirable that you remain for a while to bask in the afterglow of the Rite: to meditate and to understand deeply that you have called the attention of the Goddess to yourself, asking to grow closer to Her, both in goals and in wisdom.

The Dedication Ritual

When an inquirer is found to be suitable for the Craft, but not yet ready for admission to a coven, a ceremony called "Dedication" may be performed. The purpose of this Rite is to call the attention of the Lady and the Horned God to the individual, and specifically, to his desire to enter the Craft.

Dedication is not a formal or rigorous rite. It may be performed at any time a Priestess/Priest desires, and when the candidate feels ready to receive it. Initially, the occasion for the ceremony is solemn. The candidate should feel he is undertaking an obligation to do all that is in his power to make his way into the Craft and fully participate in it. After the ritual ends, the occasion is joyous, as the candidate has now started upon the road that will lead him to the Craft, and has acknowledged his/her beginning steps toward full participation.

All that is needed to perform the Dedication is a candle, although incense may be used if so desired. The symbolism of the Light is, in this instance, rather obvious. Light or knowledge is at the end of the road on which the candidate is embarking. In being dedicated, the candidate acknowledges that he/she is making a start on that road.

The candidate must either ask for dedication, or he may be told that he may be dedicated if he so wishes. He must, of course, agree to the dedication for it to be effective, and the rite must be done by a member of the opposite sex to the candidate, although an intermediary can serve if necessary.

Once the candle is lit, it may be left to burn out, symbolizing that once the candidate is dedicated, he or she will live out this lifetime in the dedicated state.

The lunar phase during which dedication is performed is not important, but waxing is somewhat better than waning.

Dedication has the result of impressing on the newcomer the seriousness of his undertaking the study of the Craft. Dedication of a candidate on his first inquiry into the Craft is unusual, and should not be undertaken foolishly. Usually it is better to see a candidate for a few times before the Rite of Dedication is performed. The conditions for dedication are not restrictive.

The candidate should read through the dedication completely before the ritual begins.

Candle and candleholder are at hand. They are placed on a low table at which the candidate may kneel. Copies of the rite are also placed upon the table so that the candidate may read from them.

Priestess/Priest:

> Do you wish to be dedicated
> To the Gods and to the Craft,
> That you may learn of them
> And that you may join the Craft of the Wise
> When you are ready?

Candidate:

> I do.
> Blessed Be my eyes
> That have seen this day.

Priestess/Priest:

> Blessed Be thine eyes.

Candidate:

> Blessed Be my ears
> That hear your voice.

Priestess/Priest:

> Blessed Be thine ears.

Candidate:

> Blessed Be my mouth
> That it may speak of thy blessings.

Priestess/Priest:

> Blessed Be thy mouth.

Candidate:

> Blessed Be my feet
> Which have led me in these ways.

Priestess/Priest:

> Blessed Be thy feet.

The candidate kneels in front of the altar/table and lights the candle.

Candidate:

> O Mother of All,
> Creatrix of all the Living,
> O Father of the Woodlands,
> Master of Death,
> Will you teach_____
> That I may learn of thee
> And become wise in the love of the Gods,
> Strong in the aid of all living things,
> Learned in thy arts,
> And skillful in thy ways.

Priestess/Priest:

> Beloved,
> Do you pledge yourself to the Goddess
> To love Her
> And to the Horned God
> To honor Him?

Candidate:

> Gladly do I pledge myself
> To the Goddess, to love Her
> And to the Horned God, to honor Him.

Priestess/Priest:

> Beloved,
> Do you pledge yourself to keep silent
> Of what you shall learn
> And to respect that which is taught to you?

Candidate:

> Gladly do I so pledge myself
> To the Goddess to love Her,
> And to the Horned God, to honor Him,

To keep silent of what I shall learn
And to respect that which is taught me.

Priestess/Priest:

> Then hear the Charge of The Great Mother,
> Called by all names of Power among Men,
> Before whose altars all the world
> Has approached in Reverence:

> I am the Eternal Goddess
> Yet I demand no sacrifice ...
> Rather I give to those who honor me.
> Yet I charge you, that if you would be mine
> And follow in my ways.
> You shall gather yourselves
> Once at each full moon
> And give worship to me ... your Queen.
> Each of you must recognize me
> And look at me,
> Lest you forget from whom you come
> And to whom you are called.
> If you would be mine you must honor my Charge.
> For those things I have made law
> May be dissolved by no man.
> Shall you obey this Charge?

Candidate:

> Gladly shall I obey
> The Charge of the Goddess.
> I pledge myself to the Goddess, to love Her
> And to the Horned God, to honor Him,
> To keep silent of what I shall learn
> And to respect that which is taught me.

Priestess/Priest:

> Then you shall be taught to be wise,
> That in the fullness of time
> You shall count yourself
> Among those who serve the Gods
> Among those who belong to the Craft,
> Among those who are called the Mighty Dead.
>
> Let thy life, and the life to come
> Be in the service
> Of our noble Lady.

Candidate:

> Blessed Be this time that marks my life,
> That I shall ever be a child of the Gods,
> That I shall learn of them
> And embrace them as my own.

Priestess/Priest (Making the sign of the Pentacle in blessing the candidate):

> May the blessings of our gracious Lady
> And her hearty Consort
> Ever go with thee.

The candidate arises and is led around the altar. He/she is then kissed by the Priestess/Priest and the other Initiates in attendance.

First-Level Initiation

A second level postulant can, of his and the Lady's account, initiate a first level postulant into the Faith. A man shall be initiated by a woman, and a woman by a man. After deciding that the person to be initiated is worthy of his first giant step, and after that person has expressed a desire to join his or her fate with us and with that of the Goddess and the Horned One, the initiation shall take place, either in some solitary place or within a cast circle.

If a place of solitude is chosen, the person performing the initiation shall prepare for the purification by finding a spot that is as secluded as possible and, together with the initiate, meditate for a short period of time. Walking "with the Sun" the initiator scribes a Circle around the initiate with the wand or athame, repeating this purification:

> **Blessed Be those within this circle**
> **Cleanse heart and mind**
> **That only truth be spoken,**
> **Truth only be heard...**

After a pause of thirteen heartbeats the initiator says:

> **A seeker is among us, _____,**
> **Proven by Magic,**
> **Who doth desire to attain to join**
> **With those who follow the Way**
> **Of the ancient Craft.**
> **I must remind you, though it has been said before,**
> **That this is not a matter to be taken lightly.**
> **For your immortal soul**
> **Shall thus be deeply committed**
> **To the paths of the Goddess, and our God.**
> **Do you desire to join**
> **Your destiny with the Gods?**

When the one to be so initated has answered affirmatively, the Priestess or Priest shall point the sword or athame at the heart of the noviate and say:

> **Know well that love and trust**
> **Must be freely given,**

That they may be freely received.
Know well the import
Of thine own words,
For even thy blood and thy life
May ultimately be required.
Do you desire to join
Your destiny with ours?

When the one to be so initated has answered affirmatively the Priestess or Priest shall ask the following:

Do you seek the Way
That stretches beyond Life and Death?

Will you serve the Goddess
And reverence the God?

Will you guard that which is shown you
From the unworthy?

After the Initiate has answered yes to all of these, the initiator makes the Sign of the Pentacle with the wand or the athame and says:

So be it!

When this is done the Initiator says:

In the name of the Lady
And those covenanted to Her, I place
This threefold Charge upon you:
To know the Goddess and The God;
To Love the Goddess and Her Consort,
And through the knowledge of the Way,
To serve the Goddess and The Horned One.
Do you, _____, freely accept the Charge?
Upon an affirmative answer, the Initiator says:
So be it. Blessed Be and Welcome, Dear Friend.

The Priestess or Priest lowers the athame or wand, and they embrace in greeting.

After a short pause for relaxation, the significance and uses of the tools on the altar shall be explained to the new one.

Next, glasses, horns, or goblets of wine should be poured, a libation offered to the Goddess and the God. Next all shall drink to the new initiate and then to the Old Ones.

~

Second-Level Initiation

A Priestess or Priest, or one of the Inner Court, can, of his and the Lady's account, initiate a first-level postulant into the second level. A man shall be initiated by a Priestess, a woman shall be initiated by a Priest. The candidate must have proven, to the satisfaction of the Priestess/Priest, that he/she is a serious and honest seeker of the Way, devoted to the Goddess and to the God, studying and practicing Magic to the benefit of him/herself and others.

Except in unusual cases, at least three full moons must have passed between first-level initiation and second-level initiation. Except in unusual cases, the candidate must have passed through the first three tasks of training in the "Grimoire of Shadows." Except in unusual cases, at least three of the Witches must both privately and to the coven have vouched for the candidate.

When the Priestess/Priest has determined that the candidate is fully worthy of a second-level initiation, it shall take place.

The Priestess/Priest performing the initiation shall prepare the great Circle in as secluded a place as possible, with surroundings worthy of the Magic to be performed. The Great Circle shall be cast and all the Witches prepared for ritual in the usual way.

At the start of the initiation, the Priestess/Priest calls on the candidate:

> **Thou art summoned O _____.**
> **Walk with the sun to the east of the Circle**
> **. . . and face us.**

The candidate walks deosil about the circle to the eastern side, then stops and faces west. The Priestess/Priest then directs another of the coven to hang a Magic mirror behind the candidate, and when this is done points with sword or athame at the candidate and says:

75

The time has come,
The sun has set,
The night is upon thee.

The Priestess/Priest then orders the candidate to be bound. This will be done by the women if a man is being initiated, by the men if a woman is being initiated. Using a rope of silver (or virgin white) the hands are tied behind and the rope passed three times about the body deosil and knotted. The Priestess/Priest says:

Thy limbs are useless
Thy sight dims
As thou dost pass beyond.

In the same manner as above, the candidate is thoroughly blindfolded. The Priestess/Priest then lays aside the sword and takes the wand. With the end of the wand a pentacle is drawn on the candidate's forehead, as the following is recited:

So soon as ever your mazed spirit descends
From daylight into darkness, remember
What you have suffered, here in the circle,
What you have suffered.

With the incense brazier the candidate is censed once before each of his seven psychic centers. The instruction continues:

After your passage between the worlds
While the mists of time flow past you,
The Halls of Judgement shall loom mightily before thee.
To the left hand there bubbles a black spring
Overshadowed with a great, white cypress.
Avoid this spring, for the waters of the left-hand path
Only lead thee lower.

The Priestess/Priest shall then sprinkle consecrated wine on the face of the candidate three times and continue:

To the right hand, there lies a secret pool
Alive with speckled trout and fish of gold;
A hazel-tree overshadows it. The primeaval
Serpent of Wisdom straggles in the branches,

77

Darting out his tongue. This holy pool is fed
By dripping water; Guardians stand before it.
Thou goest to the right; to the pool of wisdom . . .
And memory.

The Priestess/Priest shall then gently touch the candidate three times upon the throat and continue:

Then the Guardians will scrutinize you, saying,
"Who are you, who? What have you to remember?
Do ye not fear the flickering tongue of the Serpent?
Go rather to the spring beneath the cypress,
Flee from this pool."

The candidate shall then say (repeating after the Priestess/Priest):

I am parched with thirst.
Give me to drink. I am a child of Earth,
But of sky also, and of the Craft.
I am also of your thrice-blessed kin.
A child of the Three-Fold Queen of Witches;
You remember me, for I have been here before.
Give me to drink!

The Priestess/Priest shall then step back and continue:

Then they will welcome you with fruit and flowers
And lead you toward the ancient dripping hazel-tree,
Crying: "Thou of our immortal blood,
Drink and remember the glorious Craft of the Goddess!"
Then you shall drink.

The Priestess/Priest shall then place a goblet of consecrated wine to the lips of the candidate, and bid him to drink. Then the candidate will be turned about to face the Magic mirror, and the Priestess/Priest shall remove the blindfold and say:

Stand before the mirror
Look far back into the past ...
Look far into the depths of your soul.

For the space of thirteen heartbeats all in the circle must be still as the candidate looks into the mirror. The Priestess/Priest then unbinds the candidate and turns him to face back to the west, and proclaims:

> (For the female Witch)
> **It is the Goddess! Lo!**
> **She rises crescented.**
> **Great is Her silver glory!**

> (For the male Witch)
> **It is the God! Lo!**
> **He strides forth grim and horned,**
> **Yet, a Servant of our Lady!**

The Priestess/Priest then pours a second goblet of consecrated wine and gives it to the Initiate, with the Toast:

> **We drink to the Old Ones.**

The Initiate is then invited to join the Priestess/Priest and the rest of the coven for wine and cakes.

Third-Level Initiation

A Priestess or Priest or one of the Inner Court can, of his and the Lady's account, initiate a postulant to the third level. A man shall be initiated by a Priestess, and a woman by a Priest. After deciding that the person to be so initiated is worthy of this next giant step and after that person has expressed the desire journey further with us and to seek more deeply the Mysteries of the Goddess and the Horned One, the third-level initiation shall take place.

Except in unusual cases, at least three full moons must have passed between second-level initiation and third-level initiation. Except in unusual cases, the candidate must have passed through most Magical training in the "Grimoire of Shadows."

The Priestess or Priest performing the initiation shall cast the Great Circle. Then all the Witches to be participating shall be prepared for ritual in the usual way.

The one to be elevated to the third level shall be brought into the circle and placed standing at the west side of the circle, facing east. The Priestess or Priest stands at the North with sword or athame. A black cloth to blindfold the candidate is loosely tied about the blade and hilt of the Magical weapon. The Priestess/Priest says:

> **A seeker is among us, _____,**
> **Proven by Magic,**
> **Who doth desire to attain to high level**
> **Within our ancient Craft,**
> **And to delve within**
> **The deepest of Mysteries.**
> **Are you willing now**
> **To begin the High Quest?**

When the one to be so initated has answered affirmatively, the Priestess or Priest shall order the one to be initated to be bound and hoodwinked. She or he is then made to kneel, facing the altar. The Priestess or Priest then moves before the candidate and says:

> **In an intiation such as this**
> **You must, symbolically die ...**
> **Pass through tests and purifications of the soul,**
> **And be born once more,**
> **With new portals opened**
> **And new powers within your soul.**
> **But for now ... sleep!**

There shall be a pause of thirteen heartbeats. Then the Priestess or Priest shall then take the pentacle and press the flat, black side of it against the candidate's forehead, saying:

> **By earth is thy still and silent body covered.**
> **By earth shall thy soul be tested.**

The Priestess or Priest shall then cense the one to be so initated, then take the athame and firmly press its edge to the center of the candidate's forehead, blowing gently and silently upon the new one's face, then saying:

By air does thy spirit go forth
Into realms strange and distant.
By air shall thy soul be tested.

The Priestess or Priest shall hold a candle before the candidate's face, close enough for the new one to feel its warmth, then with the wand gently touch the candidate between the eyes, saying:

By fire, red and flaming,
And not of this world
Shall all dross be burned from thee.
By fire shall thy soul be tested.

The Priestess or Priest shall then pour some of the consecreated water into the cup, and with the aspergillis sprinkle the face and breast of the one to be so initated, saying:

By water shall all which is old and useless
Be dissolved and washed away.
With water, pure and Magical,
Does new life arise once more.
By water shall thy soul be tested.

The Priestess or Priest shall then pause for the space of thirteen heartbeats, then continue:

Now, in thy mind's eye
A vision does come forth.
Thy soul hath passed the tests
And waits in the cold darkness
Of a great, ancient, and echoing hall.
For a time all is silent.
Then before thee, on a great throne
Grows a nimbus of colored light, glowing ever brighter.
And thereupon, in brilliance and warmth,
Appears the High Queen.
She is clad in soft robes
Of deepest blue and glowing red.

Her hair is a stream of the brightest gold.
The eyes of the Lady
Are blue and shining as the sea.
She looks upon you, and through you ...
Seeing all that you have been in the past
Or shall be in the future.
She sees your hopes and your dreams,
Then smiles and gives you Her blessing.
The vision vanishes
As you are whirled away
In growing warmth and light,
For life has begun again.

The cords shall be untied and the Priestess or Priest shall then remove the blindfold, then aid the new Witch to his/her feet, saying:

So be it.
Blessed Be and welcome back, dear friend.

An embrace and/or kiss by each within the circle is appropriate at this time. Wine is poured for all and, after a small libation by each present, a toast shall be made in honor of the new Initiate of the Third Level.

The Rite of Ordination

The following rite shall be performed at the first time that a Witch assumes priestship or priesthood of a coven. It is not necessary thereafter. The ritual shall be conducted by a Priestess or Priest of the Craft, by members of the Inner Court, or preferably by the highest-ranking Priestess or Priest in attendance. A Priestess should always be ordained by a man and a Priest by a woman. Particularly if a seeker has come from far to gain an initiation and will be returning to form her or his own group, this ceremony is a very effective means of "passing the flame." It may be modified as necessary for the occasion.

Prior to the Rite, the ordaining Priestess or Priest shall place the circlet of the one to be initiated upon the Pentacle, and move it to the front of the altar. The circle shall be cast as usual, then the ordaining Priestess or Priest shall stand at the front of the altar, facing south, and shall call:

> **I do call to stand before me**
> **One who soon shall guide**
> **A coven of our ancient Craft.**

The one being ordained shall then stand before the Priestess or Priest, who shall say:

> **The high rank for which you are chosen**
> **Does require many duties and responsibilities of you.**
> **Their fulfillment is a sacred responsibility.**
> **The secrets of the Craft**
> **Shall be under your control**
> **And under your safekeeping.**
> **In the Name of our Lady,**
> **See that they are used only for good.**
> **Do you desire**
> **The office of Priestess/Priest?**

After the one being ordained has answered in the affirmative, the Priestess or Priest shall continue with the Oath of Ordination:

> **As I do hold forth my athame**
> **Place yours beneath mine, touching.**
> **And repeat after me.**
> **I, _____, in the Name of the Queen of**
> **the Universe,**
> **Do solemnly swear that I will,**
> **To the utmost of my power,**
> **Fulfill the high office for which I have been chosen,**
> **And by me accepted freely, for the good of the Craft.**
> **I shall perform the rites and observe my duties**
> **With diligence and with the care of love.**
> **This I do affirm in the Names of the Lady**
> **And of the Horned God.**
> **So mote it be!**

All:

> So mote it be!

The Priestess or Priest shall then say:

> **Kneel, I do bid you,**
> **And receive the symbol**
> **Of your Priestesship/Priesthood.**

One of the coven shall lift the Pentacle and crown and hold it before the Priestess or Priest, and beside the one being ordained. The Priestess or Priest shall dip the aspergillis in wine or water and sprinkle the headpiece, saying:

> **I do ask of the Old Ones**
> **That the one who this wears,**
> **Be led always in the paths**
> **Of the Lady, and of Her Craft.**

The headpiece shall then be put in place by the Priestess or Priest, who shall say:

> **Thy first responsibility is to the Goddess.**
> **The second is to those of thy coven.**
> **The third is to thy soul and heart.**
> **With this crown is the eternal flame passed to thee.**
> **Use it well, wherever thou goest.**
> **So mote it be!**

A kiss or salute is appropriate here, for the Rite is finished.

All will share wine and toast to the new Priestess or Priest. The newly ordained one shall perform the rest of the evening's rituals.

The Rite for Consecration and Baptism
of an Infant

Although no youth may be Initiated into the Outer Court until the age of thirteen, according to the most ancient traditions an infant may be consecrated by its mother, before the Goddess, the God, and the Old Ones.

On the first day after the mother is up and about after childbirth, she should take the infant (well-bundled for warmth) to some wild and private place, preferably at the edge of a forest or near rowan and willow trees. When none can see her, she should kneel and touch the baby's brow to the Earth, saying:

> O Mother of all
> With Thy kiss
> Wilt Thou bless my child_____.
> Grant him/her Thy wisdom
> And Thy protection.

If she is near a fresh stream, or the sea, she should sprinkle a few drops of water on the child and repeat the above, except that she shall say "baptism" instead of "kiss."

~

Initiation of a Child

An infant may be dedicated to the Goddess, the God, and The Old Ones shortly after birth. A child may be Initiated at the age of five years with a parent taking the vows for the young one—who must however, understand the meanings of the questions at the end of the rite.

The First Degree Initiation Rite shall be used, but with the following additional provisos. Insofar as possible, the entire ritual should be slanted toward the child, and carried along at a leisurely pace, even stopping if necessary to explain things if the young one has any questions. The atmosphere must be gentle and friendly, and the child must feel completely at home.

Especially fancy robes should be made up for the young one; robes which are definitely "something special." Before the rite the parents will have explained the basic lore of Magic: what it is and how it works. (This may not always be

necessary, for children usually have an excellent intuitive grasp of Magic). A small, ornate athame will be made up, which is presented to the young one during the Initiation. The parents should explain beforehand the the uses of the athame, and that it is something special that is to be used only for Witch rites, and wrapped in black cloth and put away at other times.

After the formal initiation ceremony, the Priestess/Priest shall informally explain a little of the meaning of the Magical tools on the altar.

A child is thus authorized to attend meetings as his or her parents do permit. However, it must always be stressed that the young one must always keep the secrets of the Craft, and should speak little of it to others.

Children are particularly sacred beings, as their minds and emotions are especially attuned to natural things and open to new ideas. Hence Witches who are parents should strive to be the best parents possible: giving discipline when needed, but also giving love and understanding aplenty.

A child should be given a small bit of Magical training as his/her parents see fit, and as constantly as they do deem necessary.

The use of nursery rhymes and traditional children's games is encouraged, as many of these are portions of ancient Witch rituals. This may be pointed out to the child.

At the age of thirteen, the child may ask to be re-initiated as an adult and will henceforth be considered as such.

The Rite for Dedication of an Infant

An infant may be dedicated shortly after birth, if the parents do so desire. In preparation for the rite a rush-basket cradle, or a small boat-shaped wooden one, should be set up just to the south of the altar. Gifts for the child and the parents should be brought by others of the coven. A cup of water should be consecrated.

The parents bring the infant to the edge of the circle, the mother carrying the small one. The Priestess asks:

> **Who is it that desires**
> **To enter the circle?**

A parent answers:

> **The small and holy one, _____.**

The Priestess shall direct that two of the Witches are to open the circle, saying:

> **Enter friends**
> **And place the sacred infant**
> **In the position of honor.**

The child is placed in the basket or cradle, the mother sits on the left, and the father on the right. They may be ushered to these places by the Priestess and Priest, who will stand before them. The Priest shall say:

> **We have here before us**
> **One who is new to this life.**
> **A small and holy being whom now**
> **We would dedicate to the Lady and to the God,**
> **That his life may be rich and full,**
> **And his destiny may be great.**

The Priestess shall take the cup of consecrated water and dip the middle finger of her right hand into it. This she shall touch to the center of the infant's forehead, then hold her hand above in an attitude of blessing and say:

> **In the Name of the warm and loving Mother Goddess**
> **I do give blessings, O _____.**
> **May you grow strong and wise**
> **Under her protection.**

The Priest shall then take the cup of consecrated water and dip the middle finger of his right hand into it. This he shall touch to the center of the infant's forehead, then hold his hand above in an attitude of blessing and say:

> **In the name of the sturdy and good God of the Forest**
> **I do give blessings, O _____.**
> **May you wax happy, skilled, and potent in Magic**
> **With His guidance and example.**

At this time the "gift of fertility" is prepared for presentation to the infant. The gift shall, for a boy, be a badge, image, ring or such, built around or containing an acorn motif. For a girl, the gift shall be a brooch, image, ring, bracelet or such, built around or containing a pearl. (Consecration may be done before this rite if desired.)

The Priestess places the gift of fertility on the pentacle and moves the pentacle to the front of the altar. She and the priest touch the points of their athames to the gift, and direct the rest of the coven to point their athames at it. The Priestess says:

>**As we here do point**
>**The blades of our sacred athames**
>**The powers of mind and soul**
>**Do glow forth,**
>**From our blades**
>**Into this gift of the Gods.**
>**Thou good and protecting Mother of the World,**
>**We do ask that Thou wilt take the power**
>**Which we do will into this gift,**
>**And make it Thine henceforth.**
>**Work through this, that Thy Magic and wisdom and love**
>**May ever guide the small one here before us.**
>**So be it.**

All:

>**So be it!**

If the child is a boy, the gift will be presented by the Priestess; if the child is a girl, the gift will be presented by the Priest. As the gift is presented, the following will be said:

>**This Gift of Fertility,**
>**Small and dear one,**
>**Do the Goddess and God give to thee,**
>**That thy body and thy mind and thy soul**
>**May strengthen and grow, enriching the world**
>**In all ways.**
>(The Sign of the Pentacle shall be made.)

Led by the Priestess and Priest, those of the coven shall form a line to go sunwise past the cradle of the infant to salute the small one with the athame, then kneel and present some small and useful gift to the child. The first, the Priestess, shall say:

Small and sacred one
I do give to thee the greetings
Of the elemental kingdoms,
Of worlds beyond worlds
Magic and wonderful.

She shall bow or drop to one knee and present her gift, which shall be taken by the father and mother. Next shall come the Priest who shall say:

Small and sacred one,
I do give to thee the greetings
Of all the wild creatures,
Of forests, winds and rains.
May they always be thy friends.

He shall briefly bow or drop to one knee and present his gift, which shall be taken by the father and mother.

The others of the coven shall give their own individual greetings and congratulations, and shall present their gifts as have the Priestess/Priest. They shall join the others who are sitting as the Priestess pours the wine for all. When all of the coven, and the mother and father have a cup, she shall say:

I propose a toast
To the new one of our people!
_____!
Blessed Be!

All:

Blessed Be!

All do drink, to celebrate the arrival and consecration of the small one.

~

The Rite of Calling

The time of this rite should be at midnight and at the time of the new moon. The place of the ritual should be illumined only by candles. An altar, preferably about two feet square, should be set in the middle of the ritual area: at the center of the altar should be placed a figure of the Goddess, and about the image should be placed the symbols of the four elements. At north should be a copper disc engraved with the sigil of earth, at east a similar representative of air, a similar one at south for fire, and a similar one at west for water. Other representations than these may be made if you feel that they are appropriate. A wand should be placed behind the image of the Lady, and five pink or blue candles arranged around the altar. At the feet of the Lady's image should be placed an incense brazier, and the scents of rose, apple blossom, or jasmine burned therein for the duration of the rite.

Near the incense brazier should be placed a token (or tokens) of the one to be affected: a picture, a lock of hair, a garment, or an object worn or carried by the person. Also on the altar should be placed a crystal or silver cup half filled with wine. The entire altar should be arranged symmetrically and pleasingly.

You should dress in robes which are used only for your Magical rites, or suitably "Witchy" clothing, and in a manner that would most affect or attract the subject, were she or he present.

Mix well less than one ounce of saltpeter with an equal amount of camomile and powdered incense. Place this "Magical catalyst" at the base of the altar.

To begin, you should light (moving clockwise) four candles placed at the north, east, south and west sides of the room, then light the candles on the altar. Taking the wand in your right hand and kneeling before the altar, hold the wand aloft in salute, calling:

> **O gracious and lovely Lady**
> **Of warmth, of love, of sweet desire**
> **I do beg that Thou wilt be with me**
> **Here in this place now made sacred**
> **To Thy Magical presence.**
> **Guide me in all things, I do ask,**
> **And grant me, for a time, control of Thy creatures**
> **To serve Thee better.**

Take up the symbol of earth, holding it out to the north, and tap it thrice with the wand, saying:

> O gnomes of the earth,
> Hearken to your sign, and listen
> I have a task
> For your clever hands.

Take up the symbol of air, holding it out to the east; tap it thrice with the wand, saying:

> O sylphs of the air
> Hearken to your sign, and listen.
> I have a task
> For your bright and high spirits.

Take up the symbol of fire, holding it out to the south; tap it thrice with the wand, saying:

> O salamanders of the fire
> Hearken to your sign, and listen.
> I have a task
> For your burning eagerness.

Take up the symbol of water, holding it out to the west; tap it thrice with the wand, saying:

> O undines of the water
> Hearken to your sign, and listen.
> I have a task
> For your passion and beauty.

Replace the wand and take up the cup of wine, holding it aloft with both hands, saying:

> Creatures of the elements,
> I do ask that thou wilt cast thy powers
> On the wine within this goblet.
> That it may become a potion of soft Magic,
> Drawing ever my loved one, my beloved, to me
> More and more as time doth pass.

Hold the cup aloft for the space of seven heartbeats, imagining as you do so that the lights and the vast powers of "the other far worlds" are flowing into the cup, and staying within the wine. Then lower the cup and say:

> My gracious and lovely Goddess,
> In Thy great honor, and for this dear one whom
> I desire,
> This ... do I drink.

Drink part of the wine and keep the rest. (If possible, have the loved one partake of some of this wine during the next three days, or put some of it in his/her food or drink. Sprinkle some of it where he or she will pass, and on the door of the beloved.) Sprinkle a drop or three of wine on the token(s) placed on the altar and with the wand draw a ninefold circle clockwise about them saying:

> My spell is upon you, O _____
> As my desire for you is great,
> May your need grow even greater.
> My spell is upon you, O _____
> May love blossom and sweeten
> Ever yet stronger.
> My spell is upon you, O _____
> I have set the sprites of earth, air, fire and water
> To coax you into my arms ... there to stay.

Cast a large pinch of the Magical catalyst into the incense brazier. Stand before the altar with arms outstretched, and call:

> O sprites of earth, air, fire, and water,
> Thou hast heard my charge!
> Bring _____, my loved one, to me.
> For I am a servant of the Great Goddess!

Stand thus for the space of five heartbeats, for there may be a quiet answer within your own mind. (Be honest with yourself about what you receive as an answer!)

Then sit and contemplate the tokens of your beloved for a while, concentrating strongly on your feelings of love, and this strength of love going forth and drawing the dear one to you. When you feel that enough has been done, take the wand and raise it in salute to each of the four quarters (clockwise), saying:

Thou strange and wonderful beings,
I thank you for being with me.
Now, do I send thee forth
To thine own realms.
I bid you to remember and to complete
The task which I have set before you.
Go!

Cast a pinch of the Magical catalyst into the brazier. Replace the wand and, with feeling, blow a kiss towards the image of the Goddess. Say:

Blessed and lovely Lady,
Grant me Thy aid, I do ask.
Thou knowest my heart, and my love.
Aid me . . . I do beg.

Put out the candles on the altar, and the others about the place of the rite.

You may move the altar to another place if you wish, but at each evening for at least three hours, burn a candle before the image of the Lady. Talk to Her often, and see your loved one frequently, if you can. Continue until the full moon. When it becomes obvious that the ritual has begun to work call in the elementals, as in the first part of this rite, and reward them with libations of fresh wine to each quarter. You may also put out a bit of milk for them on three successive nights, pouring out whatever remains onto a living bush at dawn.

CAVEAT: Before deciding to perform this ritual, consider well whether this rite should indeed be done. Is there a chance for success? How real a chance? Are you looking for lifelong love, or is it short-term lust? And mostly, consider the ethics of affecting another's heart and mind!

The Rite of Handfasting

It may be that a man and a woman within the Craft will desire marriage, to state their vows of love before the Goddess and to become One within Her court. If their love is honest and deep, and the Priestess and Priest know that it is acceptable before the Goddess, they may take the Rite of Handfasting.

The ritual of Handfasting is best performed at the time of the new moon, that their love may grow as the moon waxes.

The Traditional Clothing

As many particulars of this ancient rite have been lost over the centuries, full details concerning the clothing are no longer available.

Some who perform this ceremony will desire to adhere as closely as possible to the features given, and add such details as seem appropriate and proper for the clothing and for the rite which follows. Most, though, will prefer to modify the ritual to their own tastes, adding, deleting, and modifying parts as desired by those to be married. Thus, this ritual as given is to be viewed as a starting point.

The bride should be dressed in a white, spangled gown that comes to her toes. It may possibly be of Cretan design from ancient times, or khiton, or medieval, with the bodice wrapped about with scarlet or blue cord, or with ribbons or silver chain. The bosom may possibly be clasped with a single red jewel. The bridal veil, or net, should, if possible, be as long as the gown. The bride should wear a garland of flowers, and other flowers as well in her hair, her net or veil, and her gown. The old tradition of "something old, something new, something borrowed, something blue" still applies. A small, jewelled scabbard should be fashioned for her athame.

The groom should wear a dark, simple robe much like that of a monk, but slightly open at the neck with a white ruffle or scarf. A heavy leather belt, studded with metal, should be fitted with a scabbard so that the coven's ceremonial sword may be worn on his left side. A smaller leather scabbard should be fashioned so that he may wear his athame on his right side. Gauntlets of metal-studded leather will be fashioned for his wrists. During the ceremony, he should wear a metal-studded headband of leather. (In ancient times a horned helmet was sometimes worn.)

Most importantly, though, the bride and groom should dress as they desire! Variations are encouraged.

This rite, more than any, is concerned with love and with the attraction that man and woman have for one another. Thus, if the bride does so desire, she and the other women may wear the sheerest and thinnest of gowns for the performance of this ritual.

Preparation for The Rite

On the day and the evening before the rite, the bride and the groom shall not be allowed to see each other. The man shall remain with the men, and the woman shall remain with the women.

The bride shall be with her friends, to finish the making of the gown and veil, and to gather flowers to decorate the house, the room in which this rite and the Great Circle will be held, flowers for the altar, and flowers for her hair, veil, and gown. The bride shall be accompanied everywhere by her friends, the Maids of the Goddess. The Old Traditions will be maintained and enjoyed by all.

The groom shall be with his friends to finish the fashioning of his wedding equipage, to purchase food and supplies for the rite and the festivities that follow. In the evening the Merry Men will provide the groom with appropriate strong drink and suitable counsel for his last unmarried day. The Old Traditions do apply.

Just before the rite, the Maids of the Goddess and the Merry Men will see that all is in order—that the banquet is prepared, that decorations and gifts are ready, and even that the marriage bed is scattered with flowers.

Flowers shall be spread over the altar, and a cauldron of flowers placed before it. The aspergillis, used for sprinkling, may be perfumed.

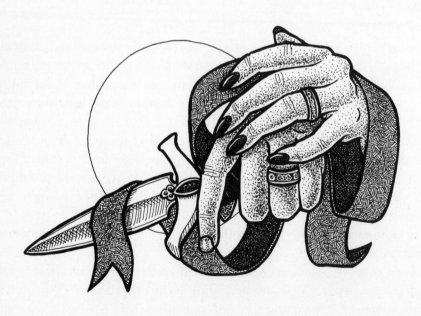

The Great Circle shall be cast in the usual manner, except that the bride shall remain out of sight with the foremost of her Maidens of the Goddess, and the groom shall remain elsewhere with the Chief of His Merry Men. The rest shall be in the circle.

The Priestess and Priest stand before the altar, and the Priest commands:

> **I say to thee, O Maiden of the Goddess**
> **And Merry Man of the Forest**
> **Open the circle . . . for two are coming**
> **Who would be one.**

The two he indicates shall open wide the Circle. If there is music it should be played at this time. The bride and groom, escorted by the Maid and the Man, approach the circle, and with a bow, the men allow the ladies to enter first. The bride stands in front of the Priestess and the groom in front of the Priest. The Priest orders the circle to be closed.

The Priestess and the Priest move to the other side of the altar, and face the Magic mirror. The Priestess says, saluting with her athame:

> **There is Magic to be done here,**
> **The Magic of love.**
> **This place is calling you, O Goddess.**
> **Come to us here from Thine own land of beauty**
> **To this holy circle, place of Thine own most pleasing.**
> **Here then, gracious Lady, bring your Lovable person;**
> **into golden goblets stir your Nectar**
> **And bless the two who here have come.**

The Priest salutes with his athame and says:

> **There is Magic to be done here,**
> **The Magic of love.**
> **This place is calling you, O Horned One**
> **Come to us from Thy wild land of sunshine and forest**
> **To this holy circle, a place of Thine own most pleasing.**
> **Here then, O bringer of joy and cheer**
> **Draw Thy rough Magic**
> **And bless these two who here have come.**

The Priestess and Priest return to their former positions. The Priest sprinkles the bride with consecrated water and says:

Thou art consecrated before the God.

The Priestess sprinkles the Groom with consecrated water and says:

Thou art consecrated before the Goddess.

The Priest then commands to both:

Kneel and receive thy charge.

The Priestess takes the wand and holds it over the top of the bride's head, saying:

Thou shalt be the star that rises from the sea
The twilight sea.
Thou shalt bring a man dreams to rule his destiny.
Thou shalt bring the moon-tides to the soul of a man,
The tides that flow and ebb, and flow again;
The Magic that moves in the moon and the sea;
These are thy secret, and they belong to thee.
Thou art the Eternal Woman, thou art she ...
The tides of all men's souls belong unto thee.
Isis in heaven, on earth, Persephone,
Diana of the Moon and Hecate
Veiled Isis, Aphrodite from the sea,
All these thou art, and They are seen in thee.

The Priest then takes the wand and holds it over the top of the groom's head, saying:

In thee may the Horned One return to the Earth again;
Hear the ancient call, and show thyself to men.
Shepherd of wild things, upon the wild hill's way
Lead thy lost flock from darkness unto day
Forgotten are the ways of sleep and night;
Men seek for them whose eyes have lost the Light.

Open the door, the door that hath no key . . .
The Door of Dreams whereby men come unto thee.
Shepherd of Wild Things, may you, one with Him be!

The Priestess tells them both to rise. She says:

It has been said that thou both
Do wish handfasting before the Goddess.
Is this so?

When they both answer in the affirmative, she says:

Draw forth your sacred athames
And place the points within the rings
That lie upon the altar.

The bride and groom do so. (Their rings lie atop one another.) The Priestess and Priest also put the points of their athames into the center of the two rings, and the Priest says:

Oh God of the Forests
Place Thy blessing
On the two Witches
Who stand before Thee
Grant unto them joy
For as long as they do desire.

The Priestess says:

Oh Lady of the Moon
Place Thy blessing
On the two Witches
Who stand before Thee
Grant unto them Magic
For as long as they do desire.

All put away their athames, Priestess and Priest upon the altar, bride and groom in their sheaths. The Priest says to the groom:

If thou dost truly desire, O _____,
To marry this woman
Give her thy weapon
That it may only be used in her service.

The groom draws his sword, and kneeling, offers it to the bride, saying:

Gracious and lovely one
Accept all that I have...
The finest
At thy service.

The bride takes the sword and hands it to the Priestess. The Priestess then says to the bride:

If thou dost truly desire, O _____,
To marry this man
Give to him thy jewel, thy crimson jewel,
For his possession as long as love shall be between you.

The bride curtseys or bows to the groom, indicating the jewel at her bosom. She looks into his eyes and says:

Thou who art handsome and strong
Accept my jewel,
My treasure
For thine own.

The groom unpins the jewel, or the bride unpins it herself and gives it to him. The Bride rises, and while they look upon each other the Priest gives each a ring and says:

Place this
Upon the hand
Of thy betrothed.

Each puts the ring on the other. They embrace as the Priestess says:

Under the blessing of the Goddess
Thy hands are fasted
And thou art one.

The Priest then calls loudly:

> **Goddess' maid and merry man**
> **Break the circle**
> **That they may depart together**
> **In the name of the Goddess!!**

As the circle is broken, the Priestess says to the bride and groom:

> **Come, let us all celebrate**
> **Your joy for the future!**

After they have departed, the circle is closed by the Priestess and the Priest as all make merry with wine and cakes and other refreshments. Singing and music should be the order of the day, and dancing as well as the wedding feast.

If the banquet is to be held among those not initiated, the members of the coven may be dressed conventionally; otherwise they may desire to change into ordinary clothing at this time. A mundane use of the consecrated sword is permitted here—it may be used to cut the cake!

The Rite for the Dead in the Circle

If one of the coven has lost a friend or a relative, this rite shall be conducted at the next sabbat or esbat, near the end of the evening's ceremonies.

At the appropriate time, the Priestess and Priest shall stand at the west and east ends of the altar, respectively, facing south toward the one who is the nearest kin or closest friend of the one who has died. If the kin or friend is a man, he shall be called forth by the Priestess, if a woman, she will be called by the Priest.

> **O, _____, we do call thee**
> **To stand here before us.**
> **That we may all honor**
> **One dear to thee**
> **Who has passed on.**

When the one is before the Priestess and Priest (others of the coven may stand nearby as well) the Priestess shall say:

> Good friend, you have for a while
> Lost one who is dear to you,
> But only for a time.
> We bid you have no sorrow ...
> There is a reason for being here
> And a reason for going.
> The Summerland is a warm and pleasing place
> With all ills gone, and youth anew.
> So let us all be truly happy
> For the one you love now knows true Joy!

Priest:

> Dying is only a mode of forgetting.
> We shall see this more easily
> If we consider forgetting
> To be but a mode of dying.

The Priestess may add more incense to the brazier at this time. She says:

> We of the Craft know when a person dies
> The soul returns again to Earth.

Priest:

> Arrayed in some new flesh disguise
> Another mother gives birth ...

Priestess:

> With sturdier limbs and brighter brain
> The old soul takes the road again.

The Priest has wine poured for all present. All do face to the north. He calls:

> O gracious Lady, and
> God of the Forest,
> We do thank Thee for guiding our friend

To the Golden Portals of the Summerland.
Convey, we do ask, the love and good wishes
   of _____,
And of the good friends here who yet remain behind.

The Priest turns to those in the circle and says:

I propose a toast ...
To the gracious and lovely Lady.
Blessed Be!

All:

Blessed Be!!

All do drink. The Priest then says:

I propose a toast ...
To the laughing and hearty God of the Forest.
Blessed Be!

All:

Blessed Be!

All do drink. The Priest then concludes:

And also do I propose a toast ...
To _____, who now revels
In the glory and the beauty
Of the Summerland!
Blessed Be!

All:

Blessed Be!

All do drink, and sit, and relax, for the Rite is over. Those in the circle shall sing, joke, and generally make merry.

~

The Rite for the Dead — Graveside

If one of the coven has lost a member of the family and desires a Craft ceremony at the interment, this rite may be performed.

If this rite is performed in a public burying ground, those of the coven may wear Witch robes over ordinary clothes if so desired. If the robes are not provided with hoods, then hooded capes shall be worn, for during a part of the ceremony, the hoods must be raised. However, it is permissible for the women to wear veil-nets if they so desire. Those not of the Craft may dress as custom dictates.

If the body lies in state before the burial, the Priestess shall see that it is properly laid out by those who are so responsible. She shall place four candles about the departed, marking the north, east, south, and west of a triple circle which shall be drawn, but not cast until later, when all have paid their respects. Only the body shall be within.

When the ceremony is to begin, the Priestess shall raise her hood, then carefully cover the body from head to toe with a net. Taking the sword, she shall mark sunwise once about the circle, saying:

> **Closed and sealed may this circle be,**
> **For the one herein must travel far ...**
> **Alone, for now.**
> **May the blessings of Our Lady speed and guide thee.**

She shall give the sword to the Priest, who shall likewise raise his hood and mark sunwise about the circle, saying:

> **Closed and sealed may this circle be,**
> **For the one herein must travel far ...**
> **Alone, for now.**
> **May the blessings of Our Lady speed and guide thee.**

He shall give the sword to the Witch who is the closest kin or nearest friend. With hood raised, the one who is the nearest and the closest to the departed shall mark sunwise once about the circle with the point of the sword, saying:

> **Closed and sealed may this circle be,**
> **For the one herein must travel far ...**
> **Alone, for now.**
> **May the blessings of those who love you**
> **Speed you on your journey.**

The sword shall be given to the Priest, who shall motion for all of the Craft who are present to assume their hoods or nets. He shall rest the point of the sword on the floor. The bereaved shall stand at his left, and the Priestess next to the left. The Priestess shall say:

> **Good friend, you have for a while**
> **Parted ways with one you know well.**
> **Though the winds of the seas**
> **Shall make your paths different,**
> **Ye shall both meet again.**

The Priest shall say:

> **All things in the universe**
> **Do go and then return again.**
> **Wheels of great stars**
> **Do turn upon themselves,**
> **The worlds return to whence they came**
> **And travel on again.**
> **The moon changes and ever repeats Her phases,**
> **The tides do ebb and flow,**
> **And life departs in one season**
> **To return in the next.**
> **So also it is with the one you have lost.**
> **The vessel now lies before us empty**
> **While the true one you have known**
> **Has journeyed to a happy and joyous place,**
> **To return again after a while.**
> **This empty shell, this empty house,**
> **Has served its owner well.**
> **Let us return it to the Earth from whence it came**
> **Our friend is free of his (or her) bonds**
> **And will return in one far better once again.**

The Priest then cuts and breaks the circle. Wine should be served before the graveside ceremony begins.

When they arrive at the burying ground, all of the coven shall be robed and hooded. Four torches shall be lit: one carried before the pallbearers, one behind, and one on either side. The Priestess and the Priest shall walk at the head of the procession, the Priest on the right, carrying the sword, and the Priestess on the left, carrying boughs of evergreen, and flowers. Others in the party should be encouraged to carry flowers also. A net shall cover the coffin.

As the coffin is placed in the grave, the Priest shall direct one torch-bearer to the foot of the grave, one on either side and one behind the Priest, Priestess, and family who all stand at the head.

When all is in readiness, the Priest shall salute with the sword to the four Cardinal Points. If it is so desired by friends and family, the Priest and/or Priestess may at this time give a brief eulogy of the departed. If singing is desired, it too shall be done at this time.

The Priest shall say:

> **Dying is only a mode of forgetting.**
> **We shall see this more easily**
> **If we consider forgetting**
> **To be but a mode of dying.**
> **There is a reason for being here**
> **And a reason for travelling beyond.**
> **Beyond the portals of the Summerland**
> **Are warmth and joy, and youth anew.**

The Priestess shall place three boughs of evergreen atop the coffin, saying:

> **As the evergreen doth grow and prosper**
> **Both in summer and in winter, year after year,**
> **So also doth the soul continue**
> **From life to life to life**
> **Growing stronger, wiser and richer.**

The Priest shall call:

> **The eye is closed: it is the smoothing of the hand!**
> **Blessed Be, dear friend. And peace be with thee.**
> **In the name of Our Lady**
> **So be it!**

He shall salute with the Sword, and all of the Craft shall make the sign of the Pentacle. Hoods shall be thrown back and veils lifted. Flowers should be strewn on and about the coffin.

All shall retire to relax, dine, and drink. Singing and merrymaking are to be the order of the day, for among Witches, death, like life, should be joyous.

The four torches should be stuck in the ground about the grave and left to burn out.

PART V

OTHER RITES AND SPELLS

Consecration of Water

When you need water that is charged Magically, for blessings, or for exorcisms, the following rite may be used. It may be altered somewhat if the situation warrants, and improvisations may be made.

Gather together your athame, an image of the Lady, and horns or other suitable representations of the God. Also get a candle and a very clean container, chalice, goblet, cauldron, or cup filled with water that is cold and very pure. Another container which is small may contain some sea salt.

Place the chalice or cup of water and the small container of sea salt before the image of the Lady and the representation of the God. The candle should be likewise placed before the image of the Lady, and lit. There should be a silent pause, no less than thirteen breaths as you become serene in your mind, putting away anything which perturbs you. Then take the athame in your right hand and touch the tip of it into the salt, saying:

> **In the Name of the Great Goddess,**
> **And the God of Strength,**
> **May all which is evil, all which is negative,**
> **All which is base and harmful**
> **Be cast forth from this creature of earth,**
> **Never to return.**
> **May only that which is good**
> **That which is clean and noble,**
> **Remain within.**
> **So mote it be!**

Take five deep breaths, feeling that you are drawing within you the pure light which is the force of life itself, and then release it through your blade as you do say:

> **In the Name of the Great Goddess,**
> **And the Great God of Strength,**
> **May this creature of earth be given power**
> **And strength, and the great forces of the universe,**
> **That in the place where it is used**
> **Only that which is good, only that which is clean and**
> **noble,**

111

And that which is secure and protecting,
May remain.
So mote it be!

Then repeat the above for the water, saying:

In the Name of the Great Goddess
And the Great God of Strength,
May all which is evil, all which is negative,
All which is base and harmful
Be cast forth from this creature of water,
Never to return.
May only that which is good,
That which is clean and noble,
Remain within.
So mote it be!

Take five deep breaths, feeling that you are drawing within you the pure light
which is the force of life itself, then release it through the blade into the water as
you do say:

In the Name of the Great Goddess,
And the God of Strength,
May this creature of water be given power
And strength, and the great forces of the universe,
That in the place where it is used
Only that which is good, and only that which is clean
and noble,
And which is secure and protecting
May remain.
So mote it be!

Then cast some of the salt into the water. Take five deep breaths, feeling that
you are drawing within you the pure light which is the force of life itself. You may
release it through your blade into the water, or hold your hands over the water in
an attitude of blessing to release the power into the water as you do say:

In the Name of the Great and Eternal Goddess,
In the Name of the God of Strength, and power and life,
May the Great Forces of the Universe

Be drawn into this consecrated water
And filling it with light ...
That it may, in any place wherein it is used,
Repel and cast forth all which is evil,
And all which is base and negative.
So that only that which is good may remain.
In the names of the Great Ones,
So mote it be!

The water may then be used, drawing with the finger or the athame the sign of the banishing pentagram where needed.

~

The Conjuration of Meal or Cakes

This rite should be used in consecrating the cakes which are ritually eaten within the Great Circle. The cakes should be shaped as crescents or as pentacles, if it is feasible.

When all is in readiness, the Priestess cups both hands over the cakes as they lie on the Pentacle held by the Priest. She says:

I conjure thee, O meal!
Who art indeed our body, since without thee
We could not live, thou who—at first as seed—
Before becoming flower, went into the earth
Where all deep secrets hide, and then when flour
ground
Didst dance like dust in the wind, and yet meanwhile
Didst bear with thee in flitting, secrets strange!
I conjure thee, O meal!
That as we take part of thee
We take part of the wisdom of the Goddess,
We learn more of the fields and the forest.
We see the ancient Way
And know the ancient lore.
So be it!

NOTA BENE: Some of the more eclectic and modern of the Craft groups honor the Lord of the Field when consecrating the meal, while honoring the Goddess through the consecration of wine. The leaders of the coven should decide which approach they prefer.

The Conjuration of the Wine

This rite should be used in consecrating the wine which will be ritually quaffed within the Great Circle.

The Cup is poured full of wine. Then the Priest holds the cup so that it is above the wine bottle, so that all the wine may be consecrated. The Priestess holds both hands over the cup and says:

> I conjure thee, O wine!
> Thou who didst grow from nothing
> By light of sun and light of moon
> The swelling, ripened grape
> The blood of the Earth pressed soon.
> I conjure thee, O wine!
> That as we drink of thee
> We drink the power of the Goddess
> Of fire, and lightning, and rain
> Of things that are wild and free!
> So be it!

Robing for the Rites

Much can be gained by making a simple ritual of assuming Witch's robes before a rite. Such a process increases your sensitivity and capability for Magic by placing your mind in a serene, dedicated aspect, and by opening up "psychic contacts" through invocation of the Great Ones. Thus when time does permit, each Witch should perform the following, or a personal ritual quite similar, before a Rite.

The first step prior to robing is to take the "lustral bath," or bath of purification. While you are in the bath, your mind should always dwell on the thought and knowledge that the water is washing away all impurities of the heart, the mind, and the soul.

After the lustral bath, lay the robe and other items out carefully. Sit for a few moments and regard your ceremonial regalia. Note that what you will be wearing has powerful symbolism behind it: the robes are a strong link with hundreds of generations of Witches, and with the most powerful Magic humankind has handled. Try to link the deepest parts of your mind with this symbolism; realize that when you put on the robes you become larger and more powerful than life: a new and nearly superhuman personality is assumed— one better and nobler. Stand and say:

> **As I do assume these robes**
> **I shall change myself**
> **To be finer, nobler, stronger,**
> **To journey between the worlds**
> **And to be with the Mighty Ones.**
> **So be it!**

If foot jewelry, toe rings, anklets, or ankle straps are worn, fasten first at the left foot, knowing that you have started on a journey to high places "between the worlds," then at the right foot, knowing that you are now committed to the Path. Say:

> **Firmly I have set my feet upon the Path**
> **Of strange Mysteries and vast powers,**
> **Through realms wild and unknown.**
> **I shall not falter,**
> **And shall return far stronger and wiser.**
> **So be it!**

You should feel that now you are able to travel anywhere—to walk unerringly across the universe in search of truth. The jewels, the metal, the leather, the ornaments in a Magical operation are nodes of psychic power, and in this way they open all ways to the Witch's feet. Yet always, as one's feet do feel the ground beneath at each step, so also does the Witch stay in contact with the world and with reality—the better to change it Magically! (There is a very ancient tradition in Europe that the key area for drawing Magical power from the Earth lies in the feet—particularly in the heel. The methods of using this knowledge have been lost, though in Oriental Magic and meditation it is usual to draw "ki," or life force up from the Earth, through the feet, and into the body.)

Next comes the robe or gown, the "Garment of Light," symbolizing the power of the Goddess wrapped about Her servant. This robe places the Witch apart from the mundane outer world, and is the symbol of the more-than-mortal being the Witch becomes within the circle. When one can finally attain the reality behind this symbol, she or he will truly be among the Great Ones.

Just before donning the robe, close your eyes and breathe in deeply five times, imagining as you do so that you are drawing in pure, brilliant white light, and that it radiates outward from within as though you were a miniature sun. As you put on the robe or gown, say:

> **As I do assume this garment**
> **I do assume a strength and a nobility**
> **Far beyond mortal bonds.**
> **The light of the Ancient Ones does shine through me.**
> **I am a new being of Magic and power.**
> **I shall be known and recognized**
> **Among the many strange and beautiful worlds beyond**
> **As one in the service of the Goddess.**
> **So be it!**

With the robe or gown about you it should seem that your aura is now intense and far-reaching. In all actions to follow, the Goddess and the God will be working through you very strongly, yet you will gain power thereby.

The cord or girdle comes next; it should be tied in a square knot or reef knot, and tight enough that you can feel its grip. The scarlet cord has always been the symbol of Witchcraft, and of the Witch's unique Magical potency. Red is the color of the blood of light; when wrapped about the waist and tied it becomes a living Magical circle with the Witch within. It is the Cord of Control, and at the same time it is the umbilical cord which binds one to the Great Mother. As the cord is tied, say:

> **Thus about me is girded**
> **The circle of strength and protection and support.**
> **Bound herein I am one with the universe outside.**
> **With this cord may I be safely guarded**
> **Through all realms,**
> **Through all strange Magics,**
> **By the Lady and the God.**
> **So be it!**

The words just spoken should then be followed by putting on the necklace for a woman and the medal, talisman, or pectoral for a man. (If she so desires, a female Witch can wear a talisman, pendant, or other jewelry in addition to her necklace.) The beaded necklace symbolizes the many lives through which we pass, one after another, in this world. Worn by a woman, it shows that all of our many lives are ultimately in the control of the Goddess-power, and to Her glory. The medallion, which should always be an amulet or symbolic of the Craft, indicates our goals, our ideals, or the Power which guides us.

When placing the necklace about her neck, the woman should say:

> **These are the many lives**
> **Of all who do live.**
> **As I do have power over these symbols,**
> **so also does the Goddess reign**
> **Over the many lives of all.**
> **And I am one with Her . . .**
> **As sister, as Friend, as Self,**
> **Sharing of Her empire.**
> **So be it!**

And the man should say:

> This is what I am, within myself;
> It is my principle, and what I shall be.
> I do ask the gracious Lady
> And my sturdy, horned and powerful comrade,
> That I may attain the reality
> Behind the symbol . . .
> The better to accomplish the vast tasks
> Which await.
> So be it!

If an additional ring is worn it should be one of sentimental value, or one used for Magical purposes. (Several may be worn, if the individual desires.) For ritual purposes a ring signifies one's own spiritual "marriage": woman to God, man to Goddess, and to the deep symbolism and power behind them. In assuming the ring, hold it before you and say, as you slowly put it on:

> As this ring fits onto my hand
> So also, in the Rite,
> Am I wedded to the Blessed One,
> To be led and guided
> By the One from whom I draw strength.
> So be it!

The Priestess and Priest shall wear as sign of their office, silver circlets, head-bands, or possibly a crown or horned/winged helmet, depending on their branch of the Craft. The pressure felt evenly about the head reminds one that Ancient Intelligences do work through the mind of a Witch. As one puts on the headgear she or he opens the deepest part of his or her mind to the guidance of the Gods. Hold the headdress in place just above the head and say:

> As I do place upon my head this crest of office,
> I do open my mind to the wills
> Of the Lady and the God.
> May they see through my eyes,
> Speak with my tongue,
> And grant me as much of their wisdom
> As my mind can know.

Lower onto the head and fit into place, saying:

So be it!

When finally you have finished the robing, pause and look at yourself in a mirror. See yourself as you should be, and as you shall be as your evolution progresses. For whether you are wearing an elaborate, floor-length robe or gown, or wearing the very minimal regalia of a dancing rite, you have now become someone far stronger, far deeper, far wiser than an ordinary person. You have become, for the rite, more than mortal.

It is best to view yourself in a full-length mirror (if possible) with the light of a single candle behind you. Say:

> **I have now stepped beyond myself**
> **And become one far nobler, far greater . . .**
> **Filled of Magic and power,**
> **Fit to journey to all places**
> **Between the worlds,**
> **Fit to share in the Empire of the Goddess**
> **And of the God.**
> **To be ever led and guided**
> **By the High Ones.**
> **Blessed Be!**

After the rite, if time does permit, it is well to disrobe in reverse order, making a quiet acknowledgement to the Powers as you do remove each item.

The Casting of the Circle
(New Version)

The circle shall be prepared as described previously. When all are within the circle and all is in readiness the Priestess (preferably) or the Priest shall take up the sword (or athame) and, starting at the eastern point, walk sunwise three times about the circle to scribe a triple circle with the sword point. As this is done, all shall visualize that the tip of the blade is setting a blue or green fire that will remain about the circle until it is broken. As the circle is scribed, the Priest shall say:

Closed may this circle be
Under the protection of the Goddess
And of the Horned God.
Protect and guide us, O Great Ones,
For all who are within
Shall be between the worlds
Until such time as it be broken.
Thrice about the circle is scribed
And thrice be it sealed!

The sword (or athame) is then replaced upon the altar.

The salutations and invocations of the cardinal points may be done by the Priestess and priest alternating, or members of the coven who have an affinity for various elements may be chosen in advance to perform this part of the rite. If the quarter candles have not been lit in advance, the individual performing the quarter salutation in each case should light the respective candle just before the words. Hold the athame out in salute, saying:

East:

Thou spirits of the air, spritely sylphs,
Elementals of the East,
We do call thee here, to be with us,
To aid in the Magic
Which we shall perform.
Blessed Be! (invoking pentagram)

All:

Blessed Be! (invoking pentagram)

South:

Thou spirits of the water, energetic salamanders,
Elementals of the South,
We do call thee here, to be with us,
To aid in the Magic
Which we shall perform.
Blessed Be! (invoking pentagram)

All:

Blessed Be! (invoking pentagram)

West:

Thou spirits of the water, graceful undines,
Elementals of the West,
We do call the here, to be with us,
To aid in the Magic
Which we shall perform.
Blessed Be! (invoking pentagram)

All:

Blessed Be! (invoking pentagram)

North:

Thou spirits of the earth, industrious gnomes,
Elementals of the North,
We do call thee here, to be with us,
To aid in the Magic
Which we shall perform.
Blessed Be! (invoking pentagram)

All:

Blessed Be! (invoking pentagram)

All do replace their athames, and the Priestess and Priest return to their places before the altar. There is a pause of nine heartbeats for meditation in silence. The Priest then crosses his arms over his chest and evokes:

Great and powerful Horned One,
Friend and protector of things wild and free,
Be with us here in this circle of Magic.
Lend to us some small portion
Of thy joy and mystery and strength.
Blessed Be!

All:

Blessed Be!

There is a pause of nine heartbeats for meditation in silence. The Priestess then holds her arms out to her sides like the limbs of the crescent moon, and evokes:

O Goddess of the Moon, and Empress of the Stars,
Thou who dost weave the fates of all things
With thy fingers of shining Magic.
Be with us here, we do ask;
Lend to us some small portion
Of thy beauty and power and wisdom.
Blessed Be!

All:

Blessed Be!

Next shall follow the consecration of salt and of water, and the blessing of each within the circle. The Priestess shall kneel before the altar, placing her hand over the salt in an attitude of blessing, saying:

Creature of earth, adore thy creatrix.
May all hindrance, and every artifice
And every illusion of evil be driven from thee.
May thou be charged with the power,
The strength and the love
Of our gracious Lady
And of her sturdy Consort.
Blessed Be! (make sign of the pentagram)

All:

Blessed Be!

Next, placing her hand over the water in an attitude of blessing:

Creature of water, adore thy creatrix.
May all hindrance, and every artifice
And every illusion of evil be driven from thee.
May thou be charged with the power,

The strength and the love
Of our gracious Lady
And of her sturdy Consort.
Blessed Be! (make sign of the pentagram)

All:

Blessed Be!

She shall then cast some of the salt into the water, saying as she stirs it with the blade of her athame:

May this salt make for strength of body
And the water make for strength of spirit.
May the place where they are used
Be made free of all hindrance and of all evil.
In the name of the Horned One
And the name of the Goddess,
Blessed Be!

Next the Priestess shall rise, taking with her the water, and proceed sunwise about the circle. On the forehead of each man she shall, having dipped her fore-finger and middle finger of her right hand into the water, draw there the invoking pentagram, saying:

Thou art blessed
Before the Goddess.

They shall exchange a kiss. The last she shall bless will be the Priest. Next the Priest shall take the water, and proceed sunwise about the circle. On the fore-head of each woman he shall, having dipped his forefinger and middle finger of his right hand into the water, draw there the invoking pentagram, saying:

Thou art blessed
Before the God.

They shall exchange a kiss. The last he shall bless will be the Priestess. Then he shall replace the consecrated water upon the altar, saying:

The circle is cast.

Now may follow the workings of the ceremony.

The Casting of the Circle
(Old Version)

The circle shall be prepared as described previously. When all are within the circle and all is in readiness the Priestess shall take up the sword (or athame) and, starting at the eastern point, walk sunwards three times about the circle to scribe a triple circle with the point, imaging in her mind that a curtain of Power is springing up as she draws the circle. She shall say:

> Closed may this circle be
> Under the protection of the Goddess.
> Protect and guide us, O Gracious One,
> For all who are within
> Shall be between the worlds
> Until it be broken.

The Priestess then replaces the sword (or athame) upon the altar, takes up the censer and censes the lines she has scribed by walking once about the circle sunwards. She then replaces the censer upon the altar.

The Priestess then picks up the Magic mirror and unwraps it. Standing at the north she holds it before her so that all of the coven may see it. She bids all to point their first two fingers of the right hand at the mirror and to gaze within. She instructs:

> Now do we breathe in, and out, deeply.
> But it is not merely air that we take in,
> It is the white, clear light which pervades the universe.
> We breathe in with our entire bodies, not just
>   our lungs
> And we breathe out pure light and life force into
>   this mirror,
> From whence its good powers will light up our circle
> So that no evil may enter.

When the Priestess judges that all have breathed five or more times to imbue the mirror with light she says:

> So be it.

The Priestess hangs the mirror at the north of the circle. She then takes up her athame and walks to the eastern point, where she faces outwards. All in the circle face with her. She points outwards with the athame and says:

> **Thou spirits of the air**
> **We do bid thee come**
> **To be about us in this circle**
> **That we may know thee better.**
> **Blessed Be!**

She salutes, and all within the circle salute and respond:

> **Blessed Be!**

The above is repeated for Fire at the south, Water at the west, Earth at the north. Then she does a final quiet salute at east.

Next follows the consecration of salt and water by the Priestess; she lays down her athame and points the first and second fingers of her right hand at the salt. Where * is indicated she makes the Sign of the Pentacle:

(Pointing first and second fingers at the salt.)

> **I exorcise thee, creature of earth**
> **By the gracious, lovely, and powerful Goddess ***
> **That thou mayest be purified of all evil influences**
> **In Her name.**

(Extending hand over salt.)

> **Creature of earth, adore thy Creatrix.**
> **In the Name of our gracious Lady I consecrate thee ***
> **To the service of the Lady, and Her Craft.**
> **So be it!**

(Pointing the first and second fingers at the water.)

> **I exorcise thee, creature of water**
> **By the gracious, lovely, and powerful Goddess ***
> **That thou mayest be purified of all evil influences**
> **In Her name.**

(Extending hand over water.)

> **Creature of water, adore thy Creatrix.**
> **In the Name of our gracious Lady I consecrate thee ***
> **To the service of the Lady, and Her Craft.**
> **So be it!**

(Casting some of the salt into the water.)

> **We pray thee, O our Goddess of things wild and free**
> **That thou mayest stretch forth the right hand of**
> **Thy power**
> **Upon these creatures of the elements and hallow them**
> **In Thy holy Name.**
> **Grant that this salt may make for health of body**
> **And this water for health of soul,**
> **And that there may be banished from the place where**
> **they are used**
> **Every power of adversity and every illusion and artifice**
> **of evil.**
> **In Thy holy Name . . . So be it!**

All:

> **So be it!**

The mixture of salt and water is now highly charged. If so desired, that which is not used may be kept for healing, exorcism, to be added to the cleansing bath prior to performing High Magic, etc.

The Priestess then takes the water and sprinkles each man, calling him by his Magical name, and stating that he is consecrated before the Goddess.

The Priest then takes the water and sprinkles each woman, calling her by her Magical name, and stating that she is consecrated before the God.

(All ritual sprinkling should be done with the aspergillis.)

The Circle is now cast.

Leaving the Circle

If for some reason it is necessary that someone leave the circle, a man and a woman will place their athame blades together and insert them together into and across the triple circle. The blades will then be spread apart so that he who desires may leave, and when he or she is passed the blades are drawn back together again. They will be left crossed and lying across the triple circle until he returns, when the circle will again be opened thus, then closed and the blades withdrawn from the circle. In no other way may the circle be opened without danger.

Dissolving the Circle
(New Version)

When the workings for the night have been completed, the power of the circle shall be released and the circle closed. The manner of casting the circle shall be repeated for the closing, with each individual who invoked a quarter now releasing that same quarter. As before, the release of the cardinal points may be done by the Priestess and the Priest alternating, or members of the coven who have an affinity for various elements to release these elements.

All shall take their athames and face to the east, holding their athames in salute as the one chosen says:

East:

> **Thou sprites of the air, elementals of the East,**
> **We do thank thee for being with us**
> **On this night of Magic.**
> **Go now to your lovely realm,**
> **And go in peace.**
> **Blessed Be!** (banishing pentagram)

All:

> **Blessed Be!** (banishing pentagram)

The candle to the east is put out. All shall face to the south, holding out athames in salute as the one chosen says:

South:

> **Thou salamanders of fire, elementals of the South,**
> **We do thank thee for being with us**
> **On this night of Magic.**
> **Go now to your lovely realm,**
> **And go in peace.**
> **Blessed Be!** (banishing pentagram)

All:

> **Blessed Be!** (banishing pentagram)

The candle to the south is put out. All shall face to the west, holding out athames in salute as the one chosen says:

West:

> **Thou undines of the water, elementals of the West,**
> **We do thank thee for being with us**
> **On this night of Magic.**
> **Go now to your lovely realm,**
> **And go in peace.**
> **Blessed Be!** (banishing pentagram)

All:

> **Blessed Be!** (banishing pentagram)

The candle to the west is put out. All shall face to the north, holding out athames in salute as the one chosen says:

North:

> **Thou gnomes of the earth, elementals of the North,**
> **We do thank thee for being with us**
> **On this night of Magic.**
> **Go now to your lovely realm,**
> **And go in peace.**
> **Blessed Be!** (banishing pentagram)

All:

Blessed Be! (banishing pentagram)

The candle to the north is put out.

All shall make a final quiet salutation to the east, then replace their athames. The Priestess and the Priest return to their places before the altar; there is a pause of nine heartbeats for meditation in silence. The Priest then crosses his arms over his chest and says:

> **Great and powerful Horned One,**
> **We do thank you for being with us here**
> **In our rite of Magic.**
> **As you depart, leave . . . we do ask . . .**
> **Some small part of thy strength and joy**
> **Within each of us here.**
> **Blessed Be!**

All:

Blessed Be!

There is a pause of nine heartbeats for meditation in silence. The Priestess then holds her arms out to her sides like the limbs of the crescent moon, and says:

> **O Goddess of the Moon, and Empress of the Stars,**
> **We do thank you for being with us here**
> **In our rite of Magic.**
> **As you depart, leave . . .we do ask . . .**
> **Some small part of thy Magic and wisdom**
> **Within each of us here.**
> **Blessed Be!**

All:

Blessed Be!

The Priest shall then take up the sword and, going to the east, proceed sunwise about the circle, cutting the circle with the blade; as he does so, all shall visualize that the circle of blue or green fire about the circle is flickering out. Then he shall replace the sword and put out the two altar candles, saying:

> The circle is closed.
> Merry meet and merry part

All:

> Merry meet and merry part.

Dissolving the Circle
(Old Version)

When the work for the night has been completed the priestess will take up her athame and walk to the eastern point of the circle, where she faces outward. All in the circle face with her. She points outward with her athame and says:

> Oh spirits of the air,
> We do thank thee for being near,
> And bid you a cordial farewell.
> Blessed Be!

She salutes, and all within the circle salute and respond:

> Blessed Be!

The above is repeated for Fire at the south, Water at the west, Earth at the north. She does a final quiet salute at the east.

She lays down her athame, walks sunwards to the mirror and takes it down, holding it before her so that all of the coven may see it. She says:

> Witches all, our night is ended.
> The spirits are departing into their strange lands . . .
> The powers about the circle are being drawn
> Into the mirror even as we watch,
> To remain there until next we meet again.
> So be it!

The Priestess drapes the mirror in its black cloth and leans it against the altar. She takes the sword and cuts the circle at East, at South, at West, at North. She then proclaims:

The circle is broken!

~

The Rite of Calling Down the Moon

Additional incense is put into the brazier. The Priestess stands beside the Magic mirror so that all in the circle may see therein. She holds her athame; pointing it at the mirror, she directs all within the circle to do likewise. She says:

> **We now point herein with the blades**
> **Of our sacred athames**
> **As we do deeply breathe in and out.**
> **But it is not just air which we take in ...**
> **It is the soft silver light of the moon,**
> **Symbol of our Lady.**
> **Each with all his body, not just his breast**
> **Does breathe in and out.**
> **And we breathe out where our blades point,**
> **The silver, clear light into this mirror**
> **That the light from this mirror,**
> **Seen by the inner eye**
> **Shall glow softly within this circle.**
> **To make this a most friendly place**
> **For our Lady's presence.**

The Priest, standing to the South of the altar, and across from her, picks up the Sword and hands it to her, saying:

> **We are the children of the moon**
> **We are born of Shining Light.**
> **When the moon shoots forth a shining ray**
> **We see within it the Goddess . . . and ourselves.**

The Priestess addresses all within the Circle:

> **What we call in our hearts**
> **Goes forth everywhere . . . echoing**
> **Beyond the stars themselves.**
> **And we need have no doubt**
> **That we are heard.**

All face to the east, holding forth their athames in salute, the Priestess saluting with the sword. The Priest says:

> **Lovely Goddess of the Bow!**
> **Lovely Goddess of the Arrows!**
> **Of all Magic and all hunting**
> **Thou who wakest in starry heaven**
> **When the sun is sunk in slumber.**
> **Thou with moon upon Thy forehead,**
> **Who the chase by night preferrest**
> **Unto hunting in the daylight.**
> **With Thy maids unto the music**
> **Of the horn . . . thyself the huntress,**
> **Queen of Magic and elfin realms**
> **And most powerful, I pray Thee;**
> **Come among us from afar, into**
> **Thy Priestess who acts as Thee.**

The salute is dropped, and the Priestess puts down the sword. The Priest motions for all to kneel, facing her. The Priestess should feel herself as one with the Goddess as she holds out her arms like the limbs of the moon and says:

> **Listen to the words of the Great Mother**
> **Who of old was called among men**
> **Artemis, Astarte, Diana, Aphrodite, Cerridwen**
> **And many other Names.**
> **At mine altars, the youth of most distant ages**
> **Gave love and made due sacrifice.**
> **Once in the month, and better it be when the moon is full,**
> **Meet in some secret place and adore me,**
> **Who am Queen of all Magics.**

For I am a gracious goddess
I give joy on Earth ... certainty, not faith while in Life.
And upon death, peace unutterable, rest,
And the ecstasy of the Goddess.
Nor do I demand aught in sacrifice ...

The Priestess pauses. She should feel that she is a vessel for the Lady, and that the Goddess speaks and acts through her. At this point she may speak further, if the Goddess within her so desires. When she is done, she will lower her arms, and the Priest shall say:

O lovely Goddess of The Moon
Fairer far than any Star
Gracious Lady, our thanks to Thee
For coming to us from afar.
We do thank Thee
For Thy warm presence
And Thy words.
Farewell, and Blessed Be.

He motions for the rest of the coven to sit, and says to the Priestess:

Wouldst my lady deign to join us?

He then stands and walks sunwards around the altar to escort her to where she will sit. Wine shall be passed about, and cakes also, if there be any.
When the time has come to close the ritual, the Priestess stands and says:

Our rite draws to its end.
O lovely and gracious Goddess of the moon
Be Thou with us as we depart.

She taps each candle with the wand before extinguishing it, starting from the north. She then calls:

The Circle is broken!
Merry meet and merry part!

All:

Merry meet and merry part!
(And merry meet again!)

Wine shall be poured and all will drink a toast to the Goddess.

A Basic Rite of Worship

The following is taken from various traditional sources and is fully in consonance with Witchcraft practices. This version is set up especially for those who are not yet initiated but are being coached and who may be considered to be "advanced students." Many variations and additions to this rite may be made. This ritual is for very limited distribution only!

The place of the meeting should be secluded and away from the eyes of strangers. It should if possible be conducted on the night of the Full Moon.

If there is singing, music and rhyme before the rite, it should concern Magick, love, and the joy of living. ("Greensleeves" is recommended.) If there is dancing, it should be in a whirling and spiralling motion by all.

A woman should be chosen to act as Priestess. She should know as much as possible about Witchcraft and occultism and, if possible, she should be most pleasing to look at. She shall choose whomsoever she desires to be her Priest.

A triple circle shall be marked upon the floor and an altar set up in the center. (Ideally, the altar should be in the shape of a cube, two feet on each side. In practice, however, a low coffee table is most frequently used.) An image of the Goddess shall be used in the center with an incense burner before it. A symbol of air shall be placed to the east, fire to the south, water to the west, and earth to the north. Candles shall be placed upon the altar and a thirteen-inch wand of black-painted willow (it may traditionally be trimmed in silver), or other consecrated wand, placed upon the altar. A broom shall be placed to the south of the altar and a double-headed axe, if available (or picture or replica), should be hung upright to the north and outside the circle. A burning candle shall be placed at each of the circle's cardinal points by the Priestess when the rite begins. Before the rite, all should bathe, "to cleanse the body and soul," and dress in clean garments—robes if possible.

When all are prepared they shall assemble within the circle. The Priestess will direct that all the candles and the incense are to be lit. Then she will have all sit, and will light each of the four candles, to be placed at the cardinal points, saying:

> **The presence of the Noble Goddess**
> **Doth extend everywhere ...**
> **Throughout the many strange, Magickal,**
> **And beautiful Worlds**
> **To all places of Wilderness, Enchantment, and Freedom.**

She places the candle at the north and pauses to look outward, saying (with all repeating after her):

> **The Lady is awesome.**
> **The Powers of Death**
> **Do bow before Her.**

She places a candle to the east and pauses to look outward, saying (with all repeating after her):

> **Our Goddess is a Lady of Joy.**
> **The Winds are Her servants.**

The same to the south:

> **Our Lady is a Goddess of Love.**
> **At Her Blessing and Desire**
> **Does the Sun bring forth Life anew.**

The same to the west:

> **The seas are the Domains**
> **Of Our Serene Lady.**
> **The Mysteries of the depths**
> **Are Hers alone.**

She sits, the Priest takes the wand and, starting to the north, draws it along the entire circle, clockwise, back to the north point, saying:

> **The Circle is sealed**
> **And all herein are totally and completely**
> **Apart from the outside world,**

That we may glorify The Lady
Whom we adore.
Blessed Be!

All:

Blessed Be!

He stands for a moment with the wand held out in front of him in salute towards the Labrys-symbol. He then gives the wand to the Priestess. She motions for all to stand and repeat after her while she holds the wand out in salute, saying:

As above, so also below.
As the universe, so also the soul.
As without, so also within.
Blessed and Gracious One,
On this day do we consecrate to Thee
Our bodies, our minds, and our spirits.
Blessed Be!

The men bow, and the women bow or curtsy.
(At this point poetry, songs, and dance—together or as individuals, yet all to the praise of the Goddess—are appropriate. Ancient Ritual from books on literature or history may be adopted for the occasion. The Priestess must approve any such suggestions.)

To close the Ritual, the Priestess stands and says:
Our Rite draws to its end.
O Lovely and Gracious Goddess of the Moon
Be Thou with each of us as we depart.

She taps each candle with the wand before extinguishing it, starting from the north. She then calls:

The Circle is broken!
Merry Meet and Merry Part!

All:

Merry Meet, Merry Part!

Wine shall be poured and all will drink a toast to the Goddess.

The General Rite of Magic

For this rite it is necessary to have a "Magical catalyst" composed of one part salt-petre and one part sugar, mixed well. If possible, some finely pulverized camomile flowers should be added. No more than one-quarter cup will be needed. This catalyst should be in a closed, and preferably ornate, glass or metal container used only for Magical purposes. Also a round card with a symbol of the item or affair which will be the Magical subject is needed. If appropriate, a picture may be used. This ritual may be performed by the Priest.

The Witch for whom the Magic is to be worked, or the Priestess, if it is a matter of common interest, will carefully explain to all present within the Great Circle what precise result or effect is sought. When all understand, the Priestess shall place the card symbolizing the subject before the incense brazier, and the container of Magical catalyst atop the card.

The Priestess then holds the sword, or her athame, so that all of the coven may see it. She bids all to point their athames at this instrument and says:

> Now do we breathe in, and out, deeply.
> But it is not merely air that we take in,
> It is the light, fine, Magical air which pervades the universe.
> We breathe in with our entire bodies, not just our breast.
> And we breathe out where we point, the light air into
>   this tool.
> In our mind's eye it fills with air … light enough to drift.
> The air shall remain herein.
> Until we release it.

When the Priestess judges that all have breathed five or more times to imbue the sword (or athame) with air-element she shall replace it so that it touches the incense brazier. She then holds the wand so that all of the coven may see it. She bids all to point their athames at this instrument and says:

> Now do we breathe in, and out, deeply.
> But it is not merely air that we take in,
> It is the bright, hot, red fire which pervades the universe.
> We breathe in with our whole bodies, not just our breast.
> And we breathe out where we point, the hot fire into
>   this tool.
> In our mind's eye we see it glowing, and feel the heat.

The fire shall remain unabated
Until we release it.

When the Priestess judges that all have breathed five or more times to imbue the wand with fire-element, she shall replace it so that it touches the incense brazier. She then holds the cup so that all of the coven may see it. She bids all to point their athames at this instrument and says:

Now do we breathe in, and out, deeply.
But it is not merely air that we take in,
It is the cold, wet, Magical water which pervades
the universe.
We breathe in with our entire bodies, not just our breast
And we breathe out where we point, the cold water
into this tool.
In our mind's eye we see the swirling green, and feel
the cold wetness.
The water shall remain herein
Until we release it.

When the Priestess judges that all have breathed five or more times to imbue the cup with the water-element, she shall replace it so that it touches the incense brazier. She then holds the pentacle so that all of the coven may see it. She bids all to point their athames at this instrument and says:

Now do we breathe in, and out, deeply,
But it is not merely air that we take in,
It is the solid, heavy earth which pervades the universe.
We breathe in with our entire bodies, not just our breast
And we breathe out where we point, the heavy earth,
into this tool.
In our mind's eyes, we see the heaviness, the solidness.
The earth shall remain herein
Until we release it.

When the Priestess judges that all have breathed five or more times to imbue the pentacle with the earth-element, she shall replace it so that it touches the incense brazier.

She then stands at the north of the altar, removes the cover of the Magical catalyst, then holds forth the card bearing the symbol of the subject of the Magic, saying:

> **The tools are charged,**
> **And lie glowing on the altar before us.**
> **Think once more**
> **Upon that which must be done.**

The Priestess then shreds the card, dropping the pieces into the container of the Magical catalyst. She says:

> **As flame and smoke do suddenly go forth**
> **So also in a flash, go earth, air, fire, and water**
> **Which we have gathered here,**
> **Charged to accomplish our desire.**

She then quickly empties all of the Magical catalyst into the incense brazier and quickly steps back to avoid the sparks. She orders wine poured for all the coven. When all are prepared she toasts:

> **Our many thanks,**
> **O creatures of the elements**
> **For thy aid.**

For the rest of the night no mention will be made of the subject of this Magic.

The Simple Rite of Magic

(For this rite it is necessary to have music which is fast and rhythmic to quicken the blood. If any of the Magical catalyst used in the General Rite of Magic is available it can be used, but this is not mandatory.)

The Witch for whom the Magic is to be worked, or the Priestess or Priest if it is a matter of common interest, will carefully explain to all present within the Great Circle what precise result or effect is sought.

When all understand, additional incense will be put into the brazier; if the brazier has a top, it shall be left open. Music shall begin and, led by the Priestess or Priest, all within the circle shall begin dancing sunwards about the circle. The dancing may be traditional, or it may be modern, it may be improvised. It is only necessary that it be fast and that males and females alternate in the line. All must bear in the back of their minds the purpose of the dance.

The dancing must continue for some time, so that all will be caught up in the speed and rhythm. As the music ends, the Priestess or Priest, whoever is leading the ceremony, will command, (in these or similar words):

> **All within**
> **The Circle ...**
> **Down!!!**

All drop to positions of rest within the circle. The Priestess or Priest kneels; if the Magical catalyst is available, a small handful of it may be thrown upon the incense brazier at this point. The Priestess or Priest stretches out both arms and calls, (in these or similar words):

> **Thou of the elements**
> **Who know our wish ...**
> **Grant it now !!!**

All relax, the men with the women. Wine is poured and the Priestess or Priest toasts:

> **Our many thanks**
> **Thou of the elements**
> **For thy aid.**

For the rest of the night, no mention will be made of the subject of this Magic.

The Magic of Knots

Any simple emotion, objective or elemental force can be tied and controlled by the simple means of binding it in a knot. Love, Magical power, winds, clouds and rain, the curing of an illness . . . all can be tied into a scarlet cord (preferably one that has been consecrated within a Great or Small Circle), then wrapped in silk and put into a box and placed in some secure location. In tradition and ancient legend, knotted cords and nets have been powerful reservoirs of Magical power.

In dealing with the elemental powers such as the wind or rain, three knots (or possibly three series of nine knots each) should be made in every case; for example, to untie one knot for a light breeze, two knots for a moderate wind, and all three knots for a gale.

Any small ritual may be composed and used in tying the knots, though the following from traditional Craft sources is often used.

THE SPELL OF NINE KNOTS

At night, when alone in some quiet place, light two candles and place them three feet apart in a north-south line. If you desire to use incense, place the brazier between the candles and about a foot to the east. Coil the scarlet cord (thirteen inches long) and place it directly between the candles at the mid-point.

With an athame or wand, draw a circle sunwise starting at the north, going three times around and ending at the north. The Small Circle thus drawn should be about five feet across, with the coiled cord at the center. When you finish drawing the circle, salute toward the north with the athame or wand.

Sit before the coiled cord, to the west of the candles. Hold the wand or athame vertically with both hands, the point touching the cord. Slowly, and deeply, breathe in and out nine times, picturing as you do so that you are inhaling pure, white light with all your body, and that as you breathe out this pure life-force flows down you through the athame or wand and into the cord, where it will stay. (For one who is beginning in Magic, this will be an exercise within the imagination. One who is sensitive or trained in Magic will see and feel the light according to his/her degree of psychic development.) Hold the athame or wand and make the Sign of the Pentacle to the east, saying:

O Gracious Lady
In Thy Name
Do I work this rite.

Take up the cord, and lay down the wand or athame in its place, with the point in the east. Bear strongly in mind the goal to be attained, while you chant the following and slowly tie nine knots in the cord.

> **This is the Number One, and the spell is now begun,**
> **This is the Number Two, thus may the spell be true,**
> **This is the Number Three, may _____ no longer**
> **be free,**
> **This is the Number Four, may the spell be**
> **strengthened more.**
> **This is the Number Five, may the spell now come alive.**
> **This is the Number Six, thus the spell be fixed,**
> **This is the Number seven, may the power through me**
> **be given.**
> **This is the Number Eight, may the power within be great,**
> **This is the Number Nine, may the spell wax strong**
> **with time.**
> **In the Name of Our Lady**
> **So may it be!**
> (Make the Sign of the Pentacle)

Put down the cord and contemplate it and the spell for a time. Then take up the wand or athame, put out the candles, stand, and cut the circle at the north, east, south and west, saying:

> **The Circle is broken,**
> **And the Spell**
> **Is cast.**

Then put the cord away in some safe place. Say nothing about the rite, and put it out of your mind for the rest of the night.

The Chant of the Year

The following is of archaic Celtic origin. On the surface it is a triple recital of the thirteen months of the lunar year. Each word, however, is the name of one of the sacred trees, which in turn each have deep philosophical and Magical implications. Additionally, the thirteen, taken in sequence, tell in rich detail the life of the Sacred King and the archaic Legend of the Goddess. All Witches should know or be strongly encouraged to study and research the hidden meanings behind this, working from the material provided by the poet Robert Graves.

Prior to commencing the chant, all shall gather in the circle, with the implications of the chant being described by the Priestess or the Priest. There shall be a pause of thirteen heartbeats while all do meditate on what has been said, then the Priestess or Priest shall intone loudly and in a rich voice, the following. The chant shall be recited with all in the circle responding, three or nine times, as deemed appropriate. It shall be closed by the final invocation. If available, incense or Magical condenser may be thrown into the incense brazier. Then all shall remain silent for a while afterwards.

Chant by Priestess/Priest with repeat by all in the circle, slowly, and sounding each letter long and resonantly:

BETH

LUIS

NION

FEARN

SAILLE

UATH

DUIR

TINNE

COLL

MIN

GORT

PETH

RUIS

Repeat three or nine times, as desired. Then close with Priestess or Priest calling:

Benignissime,
Solo Tibi Cordis,
Devotionem,
Quotidianam Facio.

Blessed Be!

~

PART VI

SEASONAL RITUALS

A Note on Seasonal Ceremonies

It often seems to those new to the Craft that seasonal ceremonies are something apart from the usual Wicca workings. Perhaps in many groups the seasonals are performed as an obligation, being a remnant of our fertility-cult ancestry.

It is true that much has been lost through centuries and millennia of neglect and persecution, but enough remains that we may have some small idea of the importance and the power that the seasonal rituals once possessed.

If one lives close to the land, the yearly cycle of the seasons becomes intimately familiar and of great mundane importance. For those who live in cities and towns, an attention to the seasonal rites can help to re-establish some contact with the Earth.

Since the most archaic times, the cycle of the year has been represented by the glyph of the eight-spoked sun wheel. There are, of course, the four major seasonal festivals and the cross quarter days that come between them. Taken as a whole, the eight yearly rituals tell the myth of a semi-divine king or hero, his dark, twin brother, and the Lady for whom they are rivals. Or they can tell of birth, life, fruition, harvest, death, and of the pilgrimage into the Lower Realms to bring back life once again.

The yearly cycle, as symbolized by the sun wheel and as told in the stories of the seasonal Witch rituals, is nothing less than a telling of the birth, life, destiny, death, and the inevitable reincarnation of all things, and an explanation of them. The rites say clearly that all things are linked through all of the world and all of the universe.

There are many levels of understanding of the seasonal rites: they speak to the highest reaches of the intellect and to the deepest realms of the subconscious. They open sources of power within the Witch that allow her or him to draw on certain fundamental energies of our biosphere.

Magical theory states that there are seasonal tides about the Earth and all things living, even extending into other dimensions and to the realms of what we would call the Gods. This cthonic/vital energy is little understood, but it seems to flow from and about certain areas on the globe, leaving in some cases those strange traces which are called "ley lines."

By a ritual which completely involves those partaking, it is possible for a coven and all its members to tap into this Power ... a sort of "Magical pumping" takes place which has many, many facets and many subtle and obvious effects.

Lady Day — Purification

Lady Day is celebrated February 2. The place of the rite should be set with flowers. The altar shall be set on the hearth, if such is available, with simply and ideally, a rose, a lily, and a sword, and with incense, candles, and cakes and wine. Numerous candles and many flowers shall be set about the periphery of the ritual area.

A period of meditation shall precede the rite. Then for a short while all shall link hands in silence for a preliminary purification. The Priestess shall call:

> **We call upon thee, O Elder Ones**
> **To be with us in this rite.**
> **Send thy friends and servants,**
> **And may they become one with us.**
> **Earth, Wind, Sea, and Fire.**
> ***Groandi!***
> ***Dynfari!***
> ***Lagastafr!***
> ***Funi!***
> **We call now upon the powers**
> **Of the elvish domains**
> **To grant us purification**
> **That we might be worthy**
> **Of their mighty Magics!**

There shall be a pause of no less than thirteen heartbeats. Then shall the Priest raise his arms and say:

> **In times long past**
> **Were the stars known as friends**
> **Of humankind.**
> **Men may forget, but the stars**
> **Are eternal!**
> **So now call we upon them**
> **As in times most ancient.**

Then shall the Priestess call:

> **We invoke thee, O sun of magnificence,**
> **Beacon of light, star of power.**

Descend thou upon us
And draw us to thee, and within thee,
That all which is base and weak
Be burned forever from us,
Leaving only that
Which is noble and godlike!

In these or similar words shall the purification be guided:

Now do we feel and sense
The drawing-nigh of vastness and power.
Now do we draw forth from all about us
The pure white light which does
Pervade the universe,
Drawing the power of light within ourselves
Through every pore of our bodies
And building a sunwise circle of power.
Growing stronger and ever yet stronger
As the ever-waxing torrent of power
Becomes a vortex
Sweeping us into the core
Of light and power titanic.
As the flow of pure white energy grows greater
It cuts through our bodies, from head to foot,
From front to back, piercing through us like a flame,
Carrying away all which is weak, all which is impure,
Leaving only that which is noble and godlike
For this rite of power.

There shall then be a period of silence of at least twoscore heartbeats while all silently allow the power so evoked to perform the purification, to crest, and to fade. Then shall the Priestess call:

We give thee greetings, O beings of enchantment,
Make clear the elvish portals,
For at this time of our blessed Lady
Shall we be worthy to enter the Holy Isle
Wherein lies the fount of immortality.

149

The Priest shall say:

> For upon this night shall our spirits journey
> To the shrine of the elvish cauldron,
> To partake of the renewing of life
> Of which the Elder Races above learned.
> This season is the time for the immortals
> To renew their powers.

The Priestess shall continue:

> For the powers of the Earth, and of the stars
> Must ever renew their greatness,
> With the life-forces which do pervade
> To the farthest reaches of the skies,
> Beyond Fagraraefr,
> And into the depths of the realms of Hel.
> At this time is the greatest of Mysteries,
> For the Crone is reborn as The Maiden,
> Troll becomes faerie,
> And age becomes youth once more!

At this time shall the Maiden Priestess (A young girl, if possible) come forward and take up the cakes, aided and guided by the Priestess in this and what follows. The Priestess shall bless the cakes, saying:

> In the wise and Magical
> Names of the Elder Ones
> And of the Gods whom we give fealty,
> May this bread of immortality
> Be blessed and consecrated.
> Blessed Be!

Then shall she bow or curtsy before the Maiden Priestess and take a cake. Afterwards shall the Priest do likewise, followed by all others in the rite. When all have partaken shall the Priest say:

> At this time is the Maiden reborn,
> Forgetting the pain and travails
> Of the weary Crone.

The waters of forgetfulness
Ease away the pain
Of that which was done
And that left undone.
Yet, deep within, wisdom remains.

The Maiden Priestess shall take up the wine, and the Priestess shall bless it, saying:

In the wise and Magical
Names of the Elder Ones
And of the Gods whom we give fealty
May this elixir of immortality
Be blessed and consecrated.
Blessed Be!

Then shall the Priest pour the wine into separate goblets and pass them to the Maiden Priestess as each in the rite does come forward, bow to her, and take a goblet. When all cups are charged shall the Priest say:

I propose a toast.
To the Elder Races!
Blessed Be! (all drink)

I propose a toast
To the Gods!
Blessed Be! (all drink)

I propose a toast.
To immortality.
As with the Elder Ones
As with the Gods,
May it be ours!
Blessed Be! (all drink)

Then shall the Priestess say:

Thus does the eternal cycle
Of birth, life, age, and death
Come full cycle ... to rebirth.

> **Thus also is the key to immortality,**
> **Fed by the star-kindling Power**
> **Of a million kinds of life**
> **Throughout the universe.**

There shall be a pause of at least thirteen heartbeats as all do meditate upon the import of what has been said. Then shall the Priest raise his right hand for the closing benediction:

> **Sain us, O Myrddin and Gwyndd.**
> **Bless us and keep us.**
> **May the elvish powers reveal**
> **Their Mysteries to us.**
> **And give us Magic, mystery, and beauty.**

There shall be a brief pause before he says:

> **This rite is ended,**
> **Merry meet, merry part!**

~

Rite for Candlemas Eve

This rite is celebrated on February 2. The place of the meeting should be decorated with berries and boughs of rowan, or mountain ash, if this is possible. If there be singing, music and rhyme before the rite, it should concern the quickening, the return of life, of new life. If there is dancing, the Priestess and Priest shall see that it is slow and sensuous. The meal before the ceremony should feature red-colored foods.

A small ship-model of archaic design should be placed on the altar for this ceremony, symbolizing the return of the Goddess after many cold months, after many cold years, and after many cold centuries. The ship should be placed on the altar between the Goddess and the God figures.

The Great Circle shall be cast in the usual manner.

To begin the rite, the Priest stands before the Magic mirror to the north of the altar, holding the ship up before him. He looks within the mirror for the space of five heartbeats and calls:

Three Ladies came out of the east
With rhyme and herbs
And iron wrought fair.
Return again, O thou White Swan,
Bride of the Golden Hair.

The Priestess, from where she sits in the Eastern part of the Circle, responds in a low voice:

The times are ill, and thou of my Craft
Shall someday make them right.
Sad the town yonder,
Sad, those that are in it;
I am the White Swan
Who shall again
Someday be Queen of them all.

The Priest, still facing the mirror, says:

I will voyage in the Lady's Name
In likeness of deer, in likeness of horse,
In likeness of serpent, in likeness of king,
To bring back the High One once again.
More powerful will it be with me
Than with all the others,
O thou gracious Goddess

All:

So may it be in thy Name.

The Rite of Calling Down the Moon shall follow. Then the rest of the night shall be spent by all in divination with the mirror, with cards, with crystals, or with other means. Blackberry wine shall be drunk.

Finally, the Great Circle shall be closed.

Lady Day/Candlemas Rite
(Alternate Version)

If an altar is used in this rite, it should be covered with a red cloth. If a cauldron is used as a centerpiece, it should be decked with red ribbons. Red and white roses should adorn the ritual area. All present should wear festive clothing, preferably in pastel colors. Three red candles and one large white candle should occupy a central position on the altar. A number of small white candles should be provided, one for each of those present, to carry in the festive procession. A bottle of sweet wine or a bottle of sweet cider shall be placed in ice near the altar, and a sacramental chalice shall be on the altar.

As the rite is about to begin, the large white candle shall be lit. All shall then link hands in meditation and purification breathing. All contemplate the meaning of Candlemas, how in ancient times the Maiden Goddess, in her fiery aspect, was welcomed back to the homes, the temples, and to the land itself in joyous celebrations on this night. How also the ancients sought to be duly purified at this time, to await the arrival of blossoming Spring.

The Priest then announces:

> **We prepare to consecrate ourselves**
> **To the honour of the Old Ones,**
> **And to welcome the blossoming Maiden.**
> **Here in this time that is not a time**
> **In this place that is not a place**
> **On a day that is not a day**
> **Between the worlds, and beyond . . .**

The Maiden Priestess then goes to the altar, lighting the three red candles. She then faces the coven, saying:

> **The Lady is come,**
> **And we welcome Her.**
> **The creatures of the wilds**
> **Know She is near,**
> **For the world shall soon feel life.**
> **The season is harsh;**
> **The Winter King rules**
> **At this bitter time . . .**
> **And this is fore-ordained.**

But now She shall return,
And life comes again,
Forest and field
Awakening in virgin purity.

The Priestess then hands to each person a white candle to carry. As this is done, a processional begins. During the processional, the Priestess chants:

Three ladies came out of the east,
With rhyme and herbs and iron wrought fair.
Return again O thou White Swan,
Bride of the Golden Hair!

Then the Priest and other members of the group take up the chant. (There are several possible manners in which this may be done. Each person could take a turn reciting the entire verse, or alternating persons might repeat different lines from the chant, or the chant may be repeated in unison.) When the procession halts, the purification follows. Starting with the Priestess and Priest, each individual in turn will approach the altar, holding his or her hands over the flames, saying:

O depths of my soul,
May I be purified!
O Threefold Goddess
Place Your warmth about me!

After this, all sit down in a circle about the altar. The Priestess takes up the goblet of honey wine and places her hands over it in an attitude of blessing, saying:

May this wine of the season to come
Be given the powers of the Lady,
New and fresh and joyous,
That we may all gain of these strengths
As we do drink,
And be blessed.
So be it!

Then she takes the wine to each individual, starting with the Priest, saying for each:

With the blessings of the Lovely Lady,
And of Her winter consort,
Art thou sustained and nourished!

As each individual sips from the goblet, she or he replies:

I drink in honor of our Ancient Gods,
To our lovely Goddess,
And to the coming seasons
Of warmth and of love.

After this ritual sacrament, the Priest kneels before the altar, with arms outspread, calling:

O Goddess and God of the ancient ways,
Spread your blessings far and wide!
And that the world may thus be led back
To the ways of peace and joy!

After this, all of the candles are extinguished. The Priest says:

The rite is ended!

A festive celebration shall follow.

~

Rite for the Spring Equinox

The place of the meeting should be decorated with boughs of alder or dogwood, if possible. If there be singing, music and rhyme before the rite, it should concern life, death and the Summerland. If there is dancing, the Priestess and Priest lead it such that the dancers whirl and spiral about the dancing place.

The candles on the altar shall be replaced by either clusters of thirteen candles each, or by a large torch in each place. Broomsticks, or stick horses, or phallus-headed sticks, shall be leaned against the altar; one shall be provided for each within the circle.

The Great Circle shall be cast in the usual manner, except that a fifteen-foot circle shall be drawn.

To begin the rite, the Priestess stands to the north of the altar with the Magic mirror behind her. She directs all within the circle to stand at the outer part of the circle, men and women next to each other. She spreads outward her arms and says:

> **Witches all, we gather now**
> **As we rise above the floods of winter**
> **To celebrate the rite of death and life.**
> **To journey in symbol nearer the Sun**
> **And out toward the darkness,**
> **Again and again,**
> **As we ourselves travel**
> **From the Summerland to this world**
> **Many times ... with many happenings**
> **Ere we reach perfection,**
> **And finally travel beyond.**

She signals for the music to start. The music should start in a slow and digni-fied manner, increasing in spirit and tempo. The Priestess rejoins the line just behind the Priest, who leads the coven in a line, starting a spiralling inward at a slow, ceremonial pace, yet with all in step or rhythm if possible. All shall chant:

> *Yan, Tan*
> *Tethera, Pethera.*

Continuing the chant and led by the Priest, they shall spiral inward and outward. Each may make his own variations in the dance, and also may follow suit with others in the circle as they turn, shuffle, stamp, in a growing and diminishing rhythm. As the music grows faster the Priest may decide to seize a broomstick, and the others will follow suit as he rides, waves, and raps the stick.

When the music is the fastest, they may leap and shout. The Priest shall lead in these usually, as all follow the spiralling in and out. Any who would rest must crouch by the altar.

The music will last for a long while. If there are any musicians, the music will end suddenly at a sign from the Priest. If the music is recorded, it will, of course, end of its own accord.

All shall drop to the position of rest. The Priestess shall stand before the altar facing north with her arms outstretched and call:

Beltiste
Soi ten cardian
Didomi cathemerios
Phylaxomenen.

All shall make the Sign of the Pentacle. If any of the Magical Condenser is available, she shall throw a small handful of it into the incense brazier.
Next shall follow the Rite of Cakes and Wine.
Finally, the Great Circle shall be closed.

Rite for Beltane

Beltane is celebrated on May 1 (May Day). The place for the meeting should be decorated with willow-boughs. A besom, or Witch's broom of willow switches, should be part of the decorations. If there be singing, music, and rhyme before the rite it should concern Magic, things new and fresh, and summer. Any dancing should be bright, energetic, and cheerful. Fencing and swordplay are traditional, the winner being crowned "King of Summer" by his lady. A Maypole should be set up and used for mildly erotic games by the ladies and men. A "Beltane Cake" containing milk, eggs, and honey should be baked; the eggshells may be saved for practical jokes, which are also traditional at this time. The atmosphere of this festival should be light, energetic, and cheerful.

Of all the festivals, this one should if possible be outdoors. If so, a Magical need-fire (actually two fires near the altar) should be struck with a flint and stone. The dancing round and between the fires would take place where shown in the rite.

A willow besom should be laid before the altar. A horned helmet or symbolic horned headdress should be set up upon the altar. If the rite is held indoors, set up two cauldrons north of the altar, far enough apart to dance between; scented oil or spirits should be added.

The Great Circle shall be cast in the usual manner, except that a fifteen-foot circle shall be drawn.

To begin the rite the Priestess stands to the north of the altar with the Magic mirror behind her. She spreads outwards her arms and says:

> Witches all, we meet on this
> The night of Walpurgis ... holy, joyous, and Magic
> To celebrate the return of the summer
> Of Life, of things new and fresh.
> I now call before me
> He who personates the God.

The Priest has the helmet placed on his head by a maiden within the Circle, and the sword placed in his hands. If they are available he should be wearing gauntlets and sword-belt. He says:

> My Lady, as the power of the God
> Is in this season supplanted
> By the warmth of the Goddess
> So also must I give honor to thee.

The Priestess gives the seasonal challenge:

> Thou hast had thy time of dominion.
> Canst thou yet stand before
> The Lady whom I represent?

The Priest replies:

> It is ordained ... I cannot.
> For cold must yield to warmth,
> And death once more to life.
> I yield to thee my power. (Salutes)

He bows and presents the sword to her. She sits on the south edge of the altar, and he ceremoniously places the helmet on her head, while she holds the sword upright as a sceptre. He says:

> To thee, with love,
> Do I yield my reign.

She motions for him to light the two fires, and proclaims:

> Thou of the joyous Craft,
> I do decree that thou dance!
> That we, and those we love

Be free in the coming seasons
Of the storms of human-kind
And the raging of the elements.
That joy of life and joy of Magic
Be ours. As I dance
So shalt thou follow.

The Priestess puts the sword and helmet down on the altar and signals for the music to start. She and the Priest lead the circular dancing, which may be formal or free-style, as they determine. In this rite there is no fixed ending to the dance; it may be as determined by the Priestess and Priest.

Next should follow the Rite of Cakes and Wine.

Dancing may follow next, if so desired.

Finally, the Great Circle shall be closed.

Rite for Midsummer's Day

The place of the meeting shall be decorated with boughs and leaves of oak, and with acorns. If there be music, singing and rhyme, before the rite it should concern sacrifice that others might live, traditions which never die, Magic, "Life continuing in spite of all," and the high spirits of one close to the elements. If there is dancing, the Priestess and Priest should lead it such that the dancers whirl about together and wheel about the dancing floor. The dances of this ritual may be performed out of the circle in practice for the rite; they should, in fact, be learned by all. Games should be played utilizing a wheel, preferably one of iron and wood, with candles or incense mounted upon it; men and ladies, for example, might play a mildly erotic game of "spin the wheel." During the rite this sunwheel should be leaned against the south side of the altar. A container of the Magical catalyst should be placed on the altar. If a labrys, or double-headed axe can be fashioned or obtained, it should be hung upright in a dominant location both before and during the rite.

Because of the large amount of lively dancing in this rite, short and light ceremonial garb of ancient Greek or Cretan style, or other very minimal but appropriate clothing may be fashioned and worn.

According to legends and traditions of the Craft, actual shape-changing of dancers sometimes occurred in this rite, especially among the Witches who were well practiced in Magic and experiencing the ecstasy of the Goddess in their Magical dancing. Only fragments of the rite survived the terrible Time of the Burnings, but this reconstruction of it is mostly complete and may again in the future be made whole through the study and practice of the modern Wicca.

The Great Circle shall be cast in the usual manner except that a fifteen-foot circle shall be used. To begin the rite, the Priestess stands to the north of the mirror with the altar behind her and says:

> **Witches all, in ages far past it was the custom on this day
> for the King who had ruled to be sacrificed in a Magical
> ceremony, that famine, storm and war would not afflict the
> people, and that the crops would grow tall and free from
> blight or drought. Darkness would be removed from men's
> souls by the courage and pride and Magic of one who, very
> willingly, walked steadily to his doom. The material rite
> was deeply emotional and rendingly impressive; yet the
> Magical portion, unseen and unseeable by human eyes was
> awesomely stronger and more far-reaching. Such Magic as
> this was cruelly powerful—but it worked magnificently!**

The Priestess sits, while the Priest stands in her place and, with his arms out in invocation, proclaims:

> On this night we gather here
> To perform again in symbol and Magical dance
> The rite of the Oak King's sacrifice,
> As it was done in ages past.
> In this day, our Lady no longer
> Requires sacrifice from any among us,
> For the life She bestows is sweet ...
> And in this season the Moon must wax.

The Priest turns to the Magic mirror, holding forth his athame in salute, calling:

> O laughing, naked Queen
> Beautiful and yet terrible,
> Thou who like all women
> Canst make and then destroy thy men
> And yet are beyond all blame ...
> For thou art the Goddess ...
> Be with us here.
> As thy holy labrys doth two edges have,
> So also, Lady, do we know that two faces dost
>   Thou have:
> One as serene, lovely, and clear as Thy silver moon,
> The other dark and awesome,
> For thou art as all women ...

The Priest salutes with his athame. If one is present who can play a reed-pipe or recorder he shall at this point play a very brief, minor-key tune as the Priestess sits on the South edge of the altar, her arms out like the limbs of the Moon, and the Priest comes to kneel before her, saying:

> Thou who above all art adored,
> Know that Thy worshippers
> Do give Thee obeisance:
> The wise, the strong, the powerful.
> And the very princes of the world
> Do give honor unto Thee.

The Priest gives her the sword, which she holds before her like a sceptre. He kneels once more and continues:

> **The Goddess is kind**
> **When it pleases Her.**
> **Thou who art the day**
> **Art also the night,**
> **And at times Thou dost require**
> **Blood and darkness and strife**
> **Among men for Thy purposes.**

The Priest stands back with the men near the edge of the circle. The Priestess stands, puts down the sword, and motions for the music to begin. The men stand fast while the women follow the Priestess five or more times around the circle, sunwise, in a slow, gracious, and stately dance. Then, led by her, they suddenly turn widdershins and dance and whirl and shout wildly back, five or more times.

Each woman returns to her man and stands, arms akimbo, while the Priestess throws a small handful of the Magical catalyst into the incense brazier. When the sparks have ceased, she seats herself upon the altar once again, saying:

> **The life of a year**
> **Is thirteen moons,**
> **With every season round.**
> **The life of the King**
> **Shall pass likewise**
> **From birth unto the ground.**

The Priestess signals for the music to begin again. The women laughingly watch the men dance sunwise around the circle, following the Priest. In the dance, the Priest chants each line (he may be prompted by the Priestess) and the men repeat, shuffling and stepping in time with the music, imitating in every manner—physically, mentally and astrally—all creatures mentioned in the King's Chant. They make one circle for each "change," the mood being light and cheerful.

> **I am a stag ... of seven tines ... for strength.**
> **I am a flood ... across a plain ... for extent.**
> **I am a wind ... on a deep lake ... for depth.**
> **I am a ray ... of the sun ... for purity.**
> **I am a hawk ... above the cliff ... for cunning.**

I am a bloom ... among flowers ... for excellence.
I am a wizard ... who but I ... brings forth the hilltop's
  Magic fire?
I am a spear ... that roars for blood ... in vengeance.
I am a salmon ... in a pool ... for swiftness.
I am a hill ... where poets walk ... for wisdom.
I am a boar ... strong and red ... for power and valor.
I am a breaker ... threatening doom ... for terror.
I am a sea-tide ... that drags to death ... for might.

All do sit as the Priest invokes:

**Who but I
Knows the secret
Of the unhewn dolmen?**

He throws a small handful of the Magical catalyst into the incense brazier at this time and sits. If it is so desired, all may drink wine and rest for a while.

When the time is right to continue, the Priestess stands with arms outstretched and calls:

**When the Queen calls, there is none
Who would not willingly come.
For Her libation must be made with love
And with pain.
And in the Magical chase
There is no transformation
Which can stay Her brassarids.**

The Priestess signals for the music to begin again. Women join in a circle at the center around the altar, facing outward. The men join in a circle near the outer edge, facing inward. The men and women, led by the Priestess and Priest, will chant and imitate in every manner—physical, mental, and astral—the creatures of the chant as they dance sunward. As the women dance, the men will stop and watch them and vice-versa.

All:

**Cunning and art he did not lack
But aye Her whistle would fetch him back.**

Men:

> O, I shall go into a hare
> With sorrow and sighing and mickle care,
> And I shall go in the Horned God's name
> Aye, till I be fetched hame.

Women:

> Hare, take heed of a bitch greyhound
> Will harry thee all these fells around,
> For I come in Our Lady's name
> All but for to fetch thee hame.

All:

> Cunning and art he did not lack
> But aye Her whistle would fetch him back.

Men:

> Yet I shall go into a trout
> With sorrow and sighing and mickle doubt,
> And show thee many a crooked game
> Ere that I be fetched hame.

Women:

> Trout, take heed of an otter lank
> Will harry thee from bank to bank,
> For here come I in Our Lady's name
> All but for to fetch thee hame.

All:

> Cunning and art he did not lack
> But aye Her whistle would fetch him back.

Men:

> Yet I shall go into a bee
> With mickle horror and dread of Thee

165

And flit to hive in the Horned God's name
Ere that I be fetched hame.

Women:

Bee take heed of a swallow hen
Will harry thee close, both butt and ben
For here come I in Our Lady's name
All but for to fetch thee hame.

All:

Cunning and art he did not lack
But aye her whistle would fetch him back.

Men

Yet shall I go into a mouse
And haste me unto the miller's house
There in his corn to have good game
Ere that I be fetched hame.

Women:

Mouse, take heed of a white tib-cat
That never was baulked of mouse or rat,
For I'll crack thy bones in Our lady's name:
Thus shalt thou be fetched hame.

All:

Cunning and art he did not lack
But aye her whistle would fetch him back.

At the conclusion, all will drop to a position of rest while the Priest says:

As one generation doth pass
And the next appear thereafter,
So Thy people always continued.
Thou hast returned to us, O Lady.
Return, we do ask, to the world outside
To bring back again the ancient ecstasy

166

**Of joy and terror
And beauty most sublime.**

He salutes with his athame as the Priestess calls:

**Achaifa
Ossa
Ourania
Hesuchia
Iachema.**

She throws a small handful of the Magical catalyst into the incense brazier and salutes with her athame. The rite is ended.

Finally The Great Circle shall be closed.

Rite for Lammas Eve

The place of the meeting should be decorated by branches of holly and, if possible, a sheaf or two of grain. If there be singing, music, and rhyme before the rite, it should concern love cut short by death, love, and sacrifice, and the "eternal triangle." If there is dancing, the Priestess and Priest shall see that it is slow and intimate. Fencing and races are traditional, with a lady consenting to be the prize for the winner, to be carried off by him for a kiss. She may want to put on a tongue-in-cheek show of grieving for the fallen or losing one.

The following may be recited by the Priestess and Priest, or it may be read aloud by various ones of the coven. In ancient times a version of this rite, or one of the legends mentioned below, were mimed ceremoniously by initiates.

The Great Circle shall be cast in the usual manner.

To begin the rite, the Priestess stands before the Magic mirror, her arms outstretched like the horns of the moon, and invokes:

> O Goddess ... friend and sister to women,
> Wife and lover to men,
> Thou who art all women,
> Be Thou among us as we know again
> This ancient wisdom,
> Sacred to Thee.

She lowers her arms and rejoins the Priest, who reads:

> Throughout this world, and others
> And the many strange and beautiful
> Worlds of the water-sprites, the wood-sprites,
> The creatures of the earth and of fire,
> In our many lives, in the lives of all others,
> In the great power of knowledge and Magic
> Of countless centuries of time . . .
> All things are cyclic.
> Kingdoms rise and fall
> And others rise from them.
> Land comes from the sea, and after aeons
> The mountains sink beneath great waves
> To rise yet again æons later.

The story remains the same,
Holding within it the greatest of truth
And the greatest of Magic.

At this point there will be a pause to add more incense. The incense brazier will be left open if any of the Magical condenser is available on the altar.

Priest:

The legends of this festival are clear:
Isis, Osiris, Set; Iduna, Heimdall, Loki;
Blodeuwedd, Llew Llaw, Gronw; and others
It is now with the year's seasons as it is with all things.

Priestess:

Now does the Goddess turn away Her face
From the lotus-born King of the Golden Cup.
Bright, handsome, and laughing though He be,
And smiles instead on His dark and somber brother
The silent, hard, and clever King of the Night.

Priest:

As season follows season, as snow follows summer,
The change is made.
For darkness must inevitably follow light.

Priestess:

As Lady Ishtar did seal the doom
Of high Gilgamesh
So also does She of the Flowers
Require the life of the smiling King.
Where falls His blood
Red flowers grow
As His immortal soul
Journeys beyond.

Priest:

> In time, in the midst of winter, He will return,
> Incarnate once again
> To know the deep love of his Lady,
> And to decree fate upon His brother.
> As day follows night,
> This must come to pass,
> For all things must rise and fall
> And only the Goddess remains the same.
> So it was, so it is, and so it shall be.

If any of the Magical condenser is available, the Priestess throws a small handful of it into the incense brazier.

Next shall follow the Rite of Cakes and Wine.

Next shall follow the rite of Calling Down the Moon.

Finally, The Great Circle shall be closed.

Rite for the Fall Equinox

The ritual area is decorated with the symbols of autumn, such as pine cones, autumn leaves, oak sprigs, mushrooms, nuts, acorns—as well as ears of grain, grape and blackberry vines, and the fruits of harvest.

If a Great Circle is cast, it is drawn in the usual or preferred manner.

The Priestess and Priest face each other from the opposite sides of the altar or cauldron (Priestess in the north, Priest in the south). The Priest says:

> The crane flies south, and winter must come.
> The green seasons are past and winds shall be cold ...
> At this balance point of the year
> The great tides of power do change.
> The Gods call upon us to look to ourselves
> And to our loved ones,
> To use well what we have gained,
> And to hold fast to all which is worthy.

The Priestess then responds:

> Now we prepare within and without
> For the seasons which lie before us.
> Strength for the spirit we now put in store
> Until the light of spring is born again,
> And the seasons of plenty return once more.

The Priestess then motions to the Priest, who moves deosil round the circle and comes to stand before her. The Priestess says to the coven:

> At a time of balance such as this
> The Divine King passes through the gates of death
> And departs for the land of rebirth.
> Tho' the candle may flame and gutter out,
> By the Gods it shall flare anew once more.

She then faces the priest, who assumes the God (Osiris) position. She invokes:

> Thou shining son of the Goddess,
> Half divine and yet half human,

171

O soul of the golden sun
Grant unto us strength, passion, joy and love.
Farewell thou, the ever returning light!
In you is life, and life is the light of man.
The Coven responds:
IO EVOHE! Hail the glorious sun!

The Priest then faces the group and says:

At this time we celebrate a season of good and plenty,
Let us then Honor the Ancient Ones!

He turns to the Priestess who assumes the Goddess Position, and invokes:

O Lady of the harvest season
Golden and beautiful as autumn.
We thank you for the season of plenty
We ask that your blessings surround us!
Bring us back again to the mystery and the beauty
Of the ancient ways!

All respond:

IO EVOHE! Hail Earth, mother of all!

At this point, the Priestess faces the coven and says:

Let the celebration begin.
All join hands in a circle dance, calling:
Blessed Be the fires of autumn!
Blessed Be the golden harvest!
Hail Earth, mother of All!
Hail the golden sun!

When the Priest deems it appropriate, he calls for the dance to halt. The Cakes and Wine ceremony is held, or a festival meal is then served.
The Circle is closed, and the rite is ended.

Rite for the Fall Equinox
(Alternate Version)

The place of the meeting should be decorated by wreaths and wrappings of grape or blackberry vines, as well as mushrooms and possibly a barley sheaf and some quince if they are available. If there be singing, music, and rhyme before the rite, it should concern drinking, celebrations, and good times. If there is dancing, the Priestess and Priest should see that it is fast, and bright, and cheerful. Pork, mushrooms, roasted apples, and wine aplenty are traditional.

The Great Circle shall be cast in the usual manner.

To begin the rite, the Priestess stands before the Magic mirror, facing it with her athame held out in salute, and invokes:

> *Alphito-Baitule Lusia Nonacris*
> *Anna Fearina Salmaona*
> *Strabloe Athaneatidas Ura druei*
> *Tanaous kolabreusomera*
> *Kirkotokous athroize te Mani*
> *Grogopa gnathoi ruseis iota.*

> **Lady of the Willows**
> **Mother of the Sacred Child,**
> **Grant to the Witches of Thy Craft**
> **An understanding of Thy mysteries.**

She drops her arms after the salute. The Priest comes beside her and also looks into the mirror, saluting with his Athame and saying:

> **Thou son of the Goddess,**
> **Half divine and yet human**
> **Whose shape did ever change**
> **Into any manner of beast,**
> **Whose body is as barley and wine**
> **And whose soul is the bright sun.**
> **Grant unto these witches**
> **Thy strength, Thy passion, Thy joy**
> **And the visions and prophecy which are Thine.**

They turn about and the Priest begins preparation for the dance, as the Priestess proclaims with cheer:

> O sweet upon the mountain
> The dancing and the singing,
> The madding, rushing flight.
> O sweet to sink to earth outworn
> To be one with the Godling
> To know all of His powers,
> To know all of His ecstasy,
> It is for this we dance:
> To know the freedom and the Magic
> Of the Horned Son of the Lady.

This dance shall be accompanied entirely by drums, starting with a strong rhythm and becoming yet faster. In addition to the drums, the Priest or one chosen by him should read and chant the following, over and again, in time to the dancing.

> O Witches come
> O come.
> Sing ye the Horned One,
> Sing to the timbrel,
> The deep-voiced timbrel.
> Joyfully praise Him
> Him who brings joy.
> Holy, all holy
> Music is calling.
> To the hills, to the hills
> Fly, O Witches
> Swift of foot
> On, O joyful, be fleet.

The music shall last for a long while. If there are drummers, the rhythm will end suddenly at a sign from the Priest. If it is recorded, of course, the finish will come of its own accord.

All shall drop to positions of rest. The Priestess shall stand before the altar, facing North, her arms outstretched. She calls:

Mete us out joy
And strength, and Magic
O knightliest one!

If any of the Magical catalyst is available, she should throw a small handful of it into the incense brazier.

Next should follow the Rite of Cakes and Wine.

Finally, the Great Circle shall be closed.

~

Rite for All-Hallows Eve

Also known as Hallo'een or Samhain, this festival is celebrated October 31. The place of the meeting should be decorated with wreathes and vines of ivy. If there be singing, music, and rhyme before the rite, it should concern death, ghosts, and Magic, yet ever return to being comforting and cheerful. The Priestess and Priest shall lead the dancing so that the dancers spiral slowly inward and outward about the dancing-floor in a cheerful manner. Traditional Hallo'een games and practices apply. A cauldron shall be featured in the decoration.

A henge of stones should be set up about the ritual circle. Brooms, willow-besoms, or riding-sticks should lie next to the altar; one shall be provided for each within the Circle. A horned helmet or symbolic horned headdress should be set upon the altar.

The Great Circle shall be cast in the usual manner, except that a fifteen-foot circle shall be drawn. The Cauldron shall be placed near the altar.

To begin the rite, the Priestess stands to the north of the altar facing the Magic mirror and invokes:

O Goddess of things living and growing
Our time of warmth and fair winds
Is ended for now.
As the day has passed
So must the night also come,
And for seven full moons
Must the dark Horned One
Have dominion.

She turns about and calls:

> **I call Thee forth**
> **O Thou who personates the God.**

The Priest stands at the South; he should be wearing gauntlets and sword-belt, if they are available. He answers:

> **I hear and come, my Lady.**
> **For as the snow must fall and winter's darkness return,**
> **So must I again resume my Power.**

The Priestess motions for him to be seated on the southern edge of the altar. She then ceremoniously places the helmet on his head, saying:

> **On this, the Holy Eve of Samhain**
> **Do I cede dominion to thee,**
> **O Horned One of the dark realms.**

She walks sunward to the front of the Priest and briefly drops to one knee, presenting him the sword and saying:

> **And for thy season,**
> **Do I cede thee power**
> **O thou of the underworld.**

The Priest holds the sword upright as a sceptre. He says:

> **I do thank thee, gracious Lady,**
> **And in my duties**
> **I shall ever owe loyalty to Thee.**

The Priestess retires, and the Priest stands, saying:

> **O thou of the ancient Craft,**
> **This night in ages past was the year's ending.**
> **On Samhain's eve were the sylphs, undines salamanders,**
> **And gnomes and sprites of the wood**
> **Free everywhere ... as they are now.**
> **On All Hallow's Eve did the mighty dead return from**
> **   their graves,**

Remembering warmth, and comfort and joy of friends.
As they do now.

The Priest removes the helmet and sheathes or puts down the sword. He says:

For all do love joy and cheer.
So therefore, Witches all, give honor and love to those
Who before us have passed into The Summerland.
Let us dance and make merry
For our comrades who have gone Beyond ...
And for our other friends from their strange
And beautiful realms. As I dance
So shalt thou follow.

The Priest signals for the music to start; it should first be fast and bright. He and the Priestess should lead the coven in a line, spiralling inward and outward. Each may make his own variations on the dance, and also may follow suit with others as they twist and turn, shuffle and stamp, in a growing and diminishing rhythm. After a while, the Priest may seize a broomstick, and others will follow suit to ride and shout and leap as the dance grows faster. In this rite there is no fixed ending to the dance; it may be as determined by the Priestess and Priest.

Next should follow the Rite of Cakes and Wine.

The rest of the night shall be spent by all in divination with the Magic mirror, with cards, with crystal, or by other means.

Finally, the Great Circle shall be closed.

Rite of Yule

The place of the meeting should be adorned with the traditional decorations of this season, with the addition of birch bark and branches. Songs, music, and rhyme may be seasonal but should all be slanted towards Witchcraft. The song "Greensleeves" is traditional and sacred to the Craft. If there be dancing before the rite, it should be bright and gay. The traditional foods are to be eaten, with the addition of pork in some form. A piece of oak-log with thirteen red candles in it should be in a central location before the rite and placed north of the altar for the ceremony. A Yule tree, fully decorated, should be placed at the north, outside the circle.

The Great Circle shall be cast in the usual manner.

To begin the rite, the Priestess stands to the north of the altar with the tree behind her. All in the circle may light the candles of those near them. The priestess shall light the candles on the log. She spreads her arms outward, her arms as the horns of the moon, and invokes:

The Ghost of the Old Year
Is with us yet.
Let us call him forth with rite and dance
Let him feast with us
And bid him farewell.
For in this season
The Sacred Child is born
Of the Goddess.
He of the Sun, who shall reign in joy
With bounteous seasons of life,
Ever rich, for all.
With song and dance
Shall we worship both ...
The Mother, ever gracious,
The Child of Promise most glorious.
Blessed Be the Goddess most noble,
The same through the ages of time
Everlasting through eternity.
IO EVOHE Blessed Be.

All do salute. The Priestess calls for fast music and all follow her and the Priest about the Circle in a fast and cheerful dance which becomes even faster. All shall chant:

IO EVOHE.
Blessed Be, IO EVOHE Blessed Be.

If the coven is carrying candles, the last one whose candle goes out as the dance proceeds shall be called "Nick," and must light candles, pour wine, and replenish the incense for the rest of the night.

At the end of the dance, the Priestess and Priest will call for all within the circle to drop to a sitting position. The Priestess shall stand before the altar facing north and say:

All Blessings
To the Lady,
And to Her sacred Child.
Blessed Be!

All:

Blessed Be!

She throws a small handful of the Magical catalyst into the incense brazier.
Next should follow the Rite of Cakes and Wine.
Before closing the Great Circle, the priest shall give the Salutation to the
Year. He shall say to those of the coven:

> **O friends of our coven,**
> **I do bid you to charge your cups**
> **And join the Salute to the Year.**

When all are holding forth their cups in salute, the Priest shall call:

> **Thirteen moons are waxed and waned,**
> **Dancing in the starry vault.**
> **Ancient year is running low ...**
> **Days of days draw to a halt.**
> **Greet the Hag and bid Her go ...**
> **Farewell to the ancient Crone,**
> **For tonight, the old guard changeth,**
> **Bid the Maiden take the throne.**
> **Rejoice, rejoice, it is reborn,**
> **The olden curse is washed away ...**
> **Shining bright the thirteen moons**
> **Shall rise to greet the newborn day.**
> **A joyous New Year! Blessed Be!**

All:

Blessed Be!

All shall drink deeply.
Finally, The Great Circle shall be closed.

~

PART VII

MAGICAL TRAINING

Magical Training

A major part of Wicca is the working of Magic. Although there are numerous methods of Magical working, it is common to all methods that one must use concentration of attention, a subtlety of the mind that can link ritual, gesture, and words with the meanings and analogies given by myth and legend, and an ability to properly touch the depths of the subconscious. The ability to fucus one's mind even to attaining trance is most useful. Master self-hypnosis. The following system has proven to be exceptionally valuable as a regimen to train and condition the mind. It adapts easily to many Magic-working methods.

~

"Seeker" Magical Training

THOUGHT DISCIPLINE

Observe your train of thoughts for five minutes while you let your mind "drift." Try to retain the whole series of thoughts and "replay" it afterwards. Record progress in your notebook.

Hold one thought, and one only, for ten minutes. Record progress in your notebook.

Keep your mind perfectly blank for ten minutes. Record progress in your notebook.

Practice all of the above until you have completely mastered them. Only then should you proceed to the next step of Magical Mental Training

INTROSPECTION OR SELF-KNOWLEDGE

If you are to master the art of Magic, you must know yourself very well; you must be conscious of the strong points of your character and the weak points thereof. Before progressing very far in this study you must know how to make use of his strengths and how to correct (or at least guard) your weaknesses. This can only be done by thoroughly and honestly looking at yourself, with no self-delusion at all. At this point you should begin making a listing in your notebook of good

My Good Points		My Bad Points	
enthusiastic	fire	tend to be lazy	earth
meditative	water	easily depressed	water
honest	earth	stubborn	earth
patient	earth	irritable	fire
etc. …			

qualities and your bad ones. Be brutally frank with yourself, for if you leave any weakness uncorrected there will be trouble later. Also, refer back to the section on theory, and note which of the four elements matches each of your traits. This can aid in correcting and strengthening yourself. Your chart should look like the sample on the following page.

Continue like this for a month or more while doing other exercises, and add to the process at any time.

CARE OF THE MATERIAL BODY

Set up a schedule of physical exercises every day, followed by a hot bath for relaxation. Continue this as long as you are training in Magic. It is very important to stay in good physical shape when working with the Mysteries. Also, set up a properly balanced diet and arrange your schedule so as to get a sufficient amount of sleep.

MYSTERY OF BREATHING

With the aid of your imagination, put a thought or idea into the air about you—the air that you will be breathing—so that, as you inhale, you literally absorb the thought or idea! The quality and not the quantity of your imagination and your thoughts is what counts in this case; you may for example use the thought that you will have a greater desire to study, a lesser desire for food or smoking, etc. Practice of this "Magical breathing" will have effect in as little as seven days. Begin on the first day with seven breaths, and increase the exercise by one breath each day afterwards. About ten minutes of practice should be sufficient. Record progress in your notebook.

CONSCIOUS RECEPTION OF FOOD

Impress ideas upon food before dining; the effect will be stronger than with the air. If possible, hold your hands in a blessing manner over the food; imagine that your thought or idea is thoroughly pervading the food. Then consume everything; do not read, but concentrate on the idea that you are absorbing. Even your health may be improved in this way. Try to make every meal a communion! Record progress in your notebook.

THE MAGIC OF WATER

Water is especially useful for impregnating with ideas or emotions. Ever since the dawn of recorded history (and probably long before) various religions have used consecrated water for Magical purposes. Water is most receptive just above its freezing temperature; it is least receptive at body temperature.

As you wash your hands imagine that you are washing all uncleanliness from your soul. Keep a record to assure regular practice.

Dip your hands into cold, or very cold, water. The magnetic-astral attractive force will draw all weakness from your soul. Keep a record to assure regular practice.

Magnetize water with an idea, as you have been doing above, then wash to absorb the idea. Keep a record to assure regular practice.

"Novice" Magical Training

PORE BREATHING

Sit comfortably in a chair or lie on a sofa, and relax all your muscles. Imagine that with each breath you take you are inhaling not only with your lungs but with every pore of your body. Be firmly convinced that all throughout your skin the vital force is being conveyed to the body; you may even *feel* the process of pore-breathing. With this exercise mastered you can increase your effectiveness in charging the air about you (more specifically you are charging the akasha) and thus "inhaling" health, success, peace, or whatever else you need most urgently. This is an important exercise which will be used extensively later. Record your progress.

RELAXATION

Sit or lie in a comfortable position and relax your body completely. Then observe yourself carefully to note any muscles which start to become restless from nerve stimulus: force such muscles to consciously relax, and do the same for any other groups of muscles which become restless, yet do not go to sleep. Complete and tranquil relaxation is your goal. Use an alarm clock, starting with five minutes the first day, then increase your relaxation period by five minutes each day until you can completely relax for half an hour. Record your progress.

BUILDING WILLPOWER

Take every opportunity to practice body control in your everyday life: if you feel tired, force yourself to do something else for a while rather than rest; if you feel hungry do not eat for an extra half hour; if you feel thirsty, do not drink for a while. Control of the body and increase of willpower will result from this Spartan regimen. No records are necessary.

You should master all the above exercises before proceeding on to the next step.

AUTOSUGGESTION AND THE SUBCONSCIOUS

The subconscious resides in the cerebellum. It is, practically speaking, an opponent, and as such must be understood, controlled, and transmuted.

When you inculcate into the subconscious a wish to break some bad habit, *omit* the concepts of space and time. If you tell it when and where the change is to take place, the subconscious will erect barriers and you will fail. Always express the wish in the imperative mood; do not *ask* something of your subconscious, *order* it!

The subconscious is the most receptive in the minutes just before you drop off to sleep. For this reason it is very important that at this time of evening you avoid being emotional or worrying.

MAGICAL TRAINING BEADS

Make up a small chain of wooden or glass beads, about thirty or forty beads in all, with a knot tied between each bead. Just before you sleep, either in an undertone or in your mind, take your string of beads and repeat once for each bead the phrase you have chosen: "I feel better each day," or "I do not like drinking," or "I'm more confident and more the master every day," until you have reached the end of the chain. Repeat this if you get up at night, and the first thing upon awakening in the morning. (A knotted scarlet cord may be used instead of the beads.) Keep a record to assure regular practice.

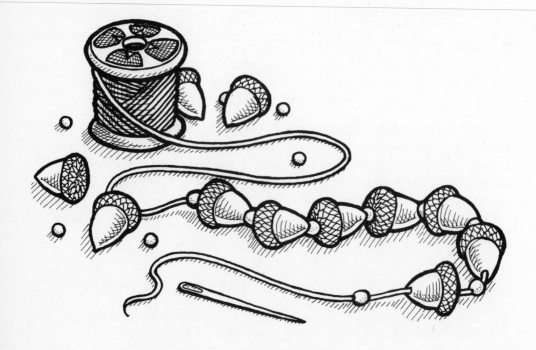

KEEPING A DREAM LOG

After a week or so of the above, begin devoting your first few minutes after awakening to recording, in a separate notebook, your dreams of the night before, as best you can remember them. Mastery of your dreams in this way not only will give you an insight into your subconscious, but is excellent pre-training for astral traveling, which is covered in a later section. A separate notebook is recommended.

MEMORY TRAINING

Place an assortment of common items, perhaps six or seven objects, on a table in front of you, look at them, close your eyes and remember one item perfectly, holding the image in your mind with its exact size, shape, and color—as though you were seeing it with your eyes closed. Try to hold the image for five minutes, noting any disturbances with your beads: one time for each time you lose the image and have to look again. Ultimately, you will be able to do this without a disturbance. Record progress in your notebook.

CREATING AND HOLDING VISUAL PICTURES

Repeat the previous exercise, but with your eyes open, so that the selected object actually seems to be hanging in the air or resting nearby, so vividly do you hold the image. Again record any disturbances or loss of the image with your beads. When you can perform this exercise for five minutes without losing your "picture" you can go on to the next exercise. Record progress in your notebook.

CREATING AND HOLDING SOUNDS

Imagine and hear the sound of a clock just as if you were in your room. Repeat with the sounds of a watch, bells, a gong; hammering, knocking, scratching, or shuffling sounds, the sounds of thunder or the wind, and the tones of various instruments. As a pleasant diversion you may want to train yourself to hear a favorite song (or several) with full musical accompaniment. Again, five minutes of continuous listening is the goal. Record progress in your notebook.

OTHER SENSATIONS

Sensory concentration: concentrate on feeling, with apparently *complete* reality, cold, warmth, gravity, lightness, hunger, thirst, and tiredness. Five minutes uninterrupted of each is the goal. Record progress in your notebook.

CONCENTRATING ON SMELLS

Olfactory concentration: concentrate on smelling the scent of roses, lilacs, and honeysuckle, then try various disagreeable smells. Five minutes is the goal. Record progress in your notebook.

CONCENTRATING ON TASTE

Taste concentration: concentrate on tasting a sweet for five minutes. Repeat with bitter, salty and acidic tastes, then with various spices. Record progress in your notebook.

You should master all the preceding before going further.

CORRECTING YOUR BAD ASPECTS

Examine again the listing you made in Step I, and to which you have continued to add. Notice particularly where you may seem to have a shortage or surplus of one element or another. Using autosuggestion as shown above, work especially hard at correcting your bad points and attaining a better mix of elements within yourself. Keep an honest record of yourself.

BUILDING AND USE OF AN ASTRAL TEMPLE

This operation requires perhaps thirty minutes initially, while resting undisturbed in a quiet place—preferably your own bedroom. Before beginning, use an athame or wand to draw a Triple Circle about the place you will be lying (moving sunwise within the circle, of course) and place a candle at each of the four cardinal points. Raise the athame or wand in salute toward the sky and say the following:

> **In the Name of the Gracious Goddess**
> **May that which is left within this circle**
> **Remain safe and secure**
> **And within Her protection**
> **While I am away.**

Make the Sign of the Pentacle. Lie down, close your eyes, and imagine that you are extending your astral body out through your pineal gland and from the top of your head. Picture yourself standing next to your body and look toward the eastern wall of the room, picturing there a door of archaic design. Within your imagination, walk to the door, swing it open, and pass through. The land you picture on the other side should be some remote place where you will be alone, yet a place where you can feel completely at home, whether it be seashore, mountains, a plain, dense forest, or whatever. Look at the other side of the entry door, noting its location: in a rock outcropping, a hillock, or a fragment of an ancient wall. Note also that through your imagination, you can array yourself in most ornate clothes, or nothing at all. Remember to hold yourself in human shape and walk one step at a time.

You may prefer to imagine that an ancient temple is already near your entryway, awaiting your use. If so, you should add a few touches with your own hands to truly make it your own. On the other hand, you may prefer (with your imagination) to grant yourself the strength of a demigod, to cut and carry and fit the stones with your own hands, building a massive stone henge or a great, classical simple hall. Light should fall upon the altar. Picture very clearly each and every detail.

When you are finished, imagine yourself standing before the altar and consecrating the temple to the Goddess with a heartfelt rite of your own composing. Then imagine quite clearly walking from the temple to the entry door, returning through it to your room, and then back into your body through the top of your head. Arise, and with your athame or wand break the circle and thank the Lady for Her protection.

Once an astral temple has been built you should use it frequently for devotional purposes and perform such rites as you desire: every evening at first, and at least every new and full moon thereafter.

At first you should physically draw the protective circle, light the candles, and invoke the Lady's protection before each journey of the imagination (and increasingly, the astral). After a time, you may forego the material ceremony and instead perform it in your imagination (or astrally) before going through the door, and again on your return.

After some practice you should ideally spend a few minutes just after going to bed and just before falling asleep, visiting your temple as described above. Try to return before falling asleep, otherwise you will probably do a considerable amount of "astral wandering" before awakening. Although this wandering is pleasant and interesting, it is wise to develop and maintain a strong self discipline in your Magical operations.

In visiting your astral temple it is well always to imagine yourself alone. Ultimately, Others will begin to appear, but such visitors must be allowed to come, and later to speak of their own accord, without any "pushing" from you. This will happen after a time, and will lead to some very rewarding and enlightening experiences.

EXERCISES WITH THE TRADITIONAL
MAGICAL TOOLS

The prime Magical tools to be found on a coven's altar are the wand, the sword (or athame), the cup, and the pentacle (often spelled "pantacle"). The uses of these tools are many and varied, and for one who is well-trained in Magic, they can yield some very powerful results indeed. The exercises which follow are intended primarily to sensitize the student and to provide a basic working knowledge of the Magical instruments; skill and power can only come through much practice.

1. Wand Exercises

At the time of the full moon cut two limbs from a willow tree: from these you should be able to make two rods, one thirteen inches long and tapering, the larger end being no bigger around than your thumb. The larger rod should be thirty-nine inches long and no thicker than two inches across at the large end. Remove the bark and trim them to be smooth; each rod should be pointed at the small end and notched at the large end (the male and female ends, respectively). If available you should paint five times with strong camomile tea, and if you desire, a small silver stickpin can be placed in either end. Carve or burn your initials at the middle. The rods may be painted as you desire. By the light of the moon, consecrate each of the wands to the Goddess with a brief prayer of your own composition. The wands are now ready for Magical use; they should be wrapped in a black silk-like material and stored away when not in use.

1.1 Thought and Meditation—At the very beginning you should work to understand very thoroughly the meaning of the term "rod" or "wand" and all it implies. In your notebook set up one or two pages with the columns shown in the chart on page 193. List all the types of rods you can and "follow through" from material objects to spiritual meanings as shown in the chart.

1.2 Attraction and Repulsion—Hold the long rod with the large end held lightly against your solar plexus with the left hand; the right hand should grip the wand about halfway out. The thumb and the forefinger of each hand should point

Subject or Symbol	Its Material Manifestation	As We Think of It	As We Feel It	Its Principle
Wand	Pen	Word	Meaning	Intention
	Match	Lighting	Illumination	Fire
	Stick	Support	Help	Aid
	Bar	Separate	Forbid	Prevent
	Chair leg	Support		
	Lamp post			

forward. The small point of the rod should be about three inches away from the wall. A soft chair should be placed behind you. Close your eyes and vividly imagine that the wand is drawing you toward the wall; in a few moments you will gently settle against it. Then repeat the process, but visualizing that the rod is repelling you; in a few moments you will lose balance and fall back into the chair. Repeat both operations several times. Perform daily for a week.

Perform the above with an imaginary (i.e., astral) wand. Perform daily for a week.

Practice the above, using a person or place as the object. Practice until satisfied.

1.3 Circling—Put some small and very commonplace object such as a vase or book or statuette in some appropriate spot within your room. With the small wand draw a single circle clockwise about it, then point the wand at the object and fill it with some very interesting quality, such as a musical tone to be heard in the mind, a faint mist about it almost visible to the eye, or a feeling of antiquity. Build strongly. In the next few days, let your attention go immediately to the object when you enter the room; rebuild the intense quality. Practice for one week.

Bring some odd, incongruous object into your room and place it in an awkward or absurd spot. Draw a widdershins (counterclockwise) circle about it, commanding, "go out, go out!" Try to feel an intense rejection. Afterward, ignore the object whenever you enter the room. The exercise is accomplished when you can stay in the room and truly not notice the object. Practice for one week.

Stand the large wand upright with the right hand, possibly resting it on some object for extra height. Close your eyes and imagine it as the central post of a spiral stairway, and walk around it as if climbing stairs. "Climb" thirty-five steps, imagining that you are ascending into someplace very wonderful. With your eyes still closed, reverse at the top and descend widdershins thirty-five steps into the "normal" world. Repeat. Practice for one week.

1.4 Preventing—Hold the large wand horizontally before you, thumbs touching, the female end at left and the male end at right. Slowly approach an open door through which the rod cannot pass. Note the feel as it checks on both sides. Close your eyes and build up a feeling of protection—as if the wand were preventing a bad fall through an open window, securely barring unwanted intruders, or keeping you and your family safe from a wild, raging storm. As you feel the physical check of the wand, and the secure feeling, say "stop." Practice until satisfied.

1.5 Banishing—Using chalk, sketch a triangle on the floor which is five feet on each side. A few feet away, and in line with a vertex of the triangle, draw a triple circle five feet across. Use the narrow end of the wand to mark out the perimeter of the triangle as you walk clockwise about it. Imagine as you move that the point of the wand leaves a glowing line behind it.

Then stand within the circle and run the wand three times about the perimeter, imagining as you do so that the tip leaves a glowing line behind it. Put the wand aside (or through your belt or sash cord) and hold your hands out before you toward the triangle in an attitude of evocation. Using your imagination, build up the image vividly of some common object within the triangle, saying, "come!" Holding the image in your mind, point the wand at it and make the banishing pentacle. As you stab through the pentacle in the final move, say, "go!" Picture vividly that a blast of pure red flame beams from the wand and totally banishes the object. Repeat the exercise. Practice very frequently.

Repeat the above, but evoke the image with the wand, using the invoking pentacle. Practice very frequently

NOTA BENE: Care should be taken not to use the image of a person or any living thing. These exercises can be of great psychic and therapeutic value, however, when used against symbolic images of one's own imperfections.

1.6 *Passing*—Hold the rod in the doorway as in the previous exercise, then switch one hand so that both thumbs point to the same end. Close your eyes and swing the wand parallel to the body. Say, "Proceed in Peace," and pass through the door slowly. Repeat. (Continue until satisfied.)

Repeat the above, but step back as if inviting a well-liked and very good friend into your home, saying, "You are Blessed and Welcome." Repeat. Continue until satisfied.

2. Sword Exercises

Obtain a double-edged sword—an old one is preferable. If none is available, construct a temporary practice one of wood. Clean it thoroughly and etch your initials in very small letters on the grip or pommel. Wipe on a thin coat of oil to preserve the metal. By the light of the next full moon, consecrate the sword to the Goddess with a brief prayer of your own composition. The sword is then ready for use; it should be sheathed or wrapped in black cloth when not in use.

2.1 *Thought and Meditation*—At the very beginning you should work to understand very thoroughly the essence of what is meant by "sword," and all that it implies. In your notebook set up one or two pages with the columns as you did in the previous section. List all of the types of sword-like things you can think of and "follow through" from material objects to spiritual meanings as you did before.

2.2 *Control in Invoking and Banishing*—Stand at attention facing east, holding the sword in the right hand, with the point directed at the ground. With your arm straight, raise the sword and make the Invoking Pentacle as shown on page 201, starting at the top and cutting with the *edge* of the blade in each direction. Say and picture vividly, "Earth, fire, life, water, air," as you cut each side. Then draw the sword back and pierce through the center of the pentacle, saying, "Come." Repeat five times, a bit faster each time. Lower the point, close your eyes and with your mind as nearly blank as possible, resonate a steady, "Hmmmmmm ... " Repeat the above, but draw the Banishing Pentacle as shown, finishing each sequence with "Go." Repeat five times, then lower the sword and resonate as before. Increase your speed.

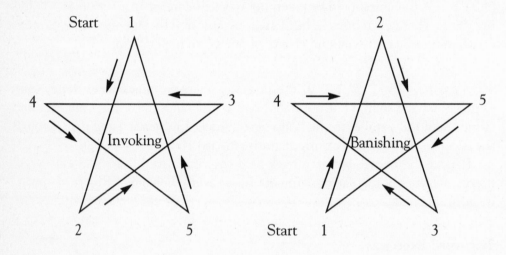

2.3 *Being Guided*—Suspend just below eye level a ring of wood or wire, which has an opening one and one-half inches in diameter. About ten feet away place a lighted candle, with the flame at the same level. Stand in a slight crouch, with your right shoulder toward the candle, and in such a position that you can see the flame through the ring. When you raise the sword, with arm straight, the point should be about seven inches from the ring. With the sword, salute the divine aspect of the Goddess which the Flame symbolizes. Point the sword again toward the flame, with your arm straight; lunge forward slowly, imagining that the circle is a portal, a hole in Existence itself. Feel that a greater Presence is drawing you on, and reduce yourself to a minimum. (This is very similar to the Zen concept of "effortless effort!") If your thrust is "good" and the point passes through the ring, withdraw the sword, return to the position of attention, and recognize the Magnificence of the Lady in the salute. If you miss, return to the position of attention and bring the sword down so that the point rests on the ground. Clasp both hands on the hilt and bow your head, thinking that, "The fault can lie only in myself. May the Divine One grant me the power of perfection." Repeat. Practice frequently for a week.

2.4 Banishing—Using chalk, sketch a triangle on the floor which is five feet on each side. A few feet away, and in line with a vertex of the triangle, draw a triple circle five feet across. Use the point of the sword to mark out the perimeter of the triangle as you walk clockwise about it. Imagine as you move the point that it leaves a glowing trail behind it. Then stand within the triple circle and run the point three times clockwise about the perimeter, imagining as you do so that the point leaves a glowing line behind it. Set the sword aside and hold your hands out toward the triangle in an attitude of Evocation. Using your imagination, build up an image vividly of some common object within the triangle, saying, "Come." Holding the image, pick up the sword, pointing it at the vivid image, saying, "Go!" Picture that a blast of clear blue shimmers from the sword blade and totally banishes the object. Repeat the exercise. Frequently, the athame should be used in place of the sword. Practice frequently.

Repeat the above, but evoke the image with the sword, using the invoking pentacle; again, an athame should be used frequently. Practice frequently.

NOTA BENE: Care should be taken not to use the image of any person or any living thing. These exercises can be of great psychic and therapeutic value, however, when used against symbolic images of one's own repressions and phobias.

3. Cup Exercises

Obtain a goblet for your use. It should be of silver if possible. Wash and polish it thoroughly, then by the light of the full moon rinse it in clear, cold water, hold the goblet up to the moon, and consecrate it to the Goddess with a brief prayer of your own composition. The cup is now ready for Magical use and henceforth should not be used for any mundane purpose.

3.1 Thought and Meditation—At the very beginning you should work to understand very thoroughly the essence of what is meant by "cup" and all it implies. In your notebook put down all types of cup which come to mind, and all which a cup can do. For example:

A cup may be:

ocean	cave	ship
human body	womb	buoy to mark the way
blood vessels	tomb	bottle with message
the heart	etc. ...	can of food for sustenance

The contents of a cup may:

be poured out	comfort	pledge or dedicate	embitter
nurture	cheer	intoxicate	poison
refresh	warm	heal	slay

3.2 *Filling and Emptying*—Hold the empty silver cup in the moonlight so that it seems to be filled with the light. Look steadily into the cup for several minutes and note that the light will swirl and pulse like a material thing. Fix in your mind that it is indeed the "living moonlight." Look carefully and dip a wand or athame into the cup to see if any of the light is "dipped up" on the tip. Try pouring out the moonlight. Repeat on five nights.

3.3 *Libation and Toast*—Fill the cup with cold water and look into it, "charging" the cup with five breaths of life-force (akasha). Hold it out with your right hand and picture vividly before you an indefinite, glowing aura of "god-force," and that the water itself within the cup is glowing slightly. Tip the cup and pour out some of the water, saying, "Do what thou wilt," and visualizing much of the akasha separating at this time, drifting in a glowing mist from the falling droplets and being absorbed into the nimbus of the god-force. (You may actually feel a definite response) Drink the rest of the water, picturing the remaining akasha being absorbed directly into your blood, and feel the vitalizing effect. Discharge or use the akasha with the appropriate breathing exercises. Repeat on seven nights.

3.4 *Singing Down the Moon*—This is a simple but valuable exercise of great antiquity. Fill the silver cup with milk and sit alone in some quiet, moonlit place. Gaze steadily at the image of the moon in the cup, humming "Greensleeves" or some other song which is sacred to the Craft. Other images will eventually appear of their own accord. Observe them. (This is a simple and useful method of scrying and can be used often.) Practice for several nights.

4. Pentacle Exercises

Fashion a metal shield two feet in diameter and perfectly circular. If metal is not available then wood may be used. Clean it thoroughly, dry and paint it: one side should be flat black, and the other side a flat white. By the light of the full moon, consecrate it to the Goddess with a brief prayer of your own composition. The shield or pentacle is now ready for use: it should be wrapped in a soft black cloth when not in use.

4.1 Thought and Meditation—At the very beginning you should work to understand thoroughly the essence of what is meant by "pentacle" and "shield," and the many ways it can control the earth element. In your notebook put down the types of shields which come to mind, and all actions that these various types of shields can perform. For example:

A pentacle or shield may be:

spoon	a lid	spade	artist's canvas
plate	jar top	hoe	printer's press
tray	table top	bulldozer	potter's wheel
sheet of paper	walls	steam shovel	TV screen
signboard	coins	dump truck	etc...

4.2 Forming—Hang the shield on the wall, black side out, a normal arm's reach away, and at eye level. The lighting should be dim; a single candle a few feet behind you would be ideal. Take your silver cup and peer into it for a while, imagining vividly that it is filled with a pure white, "liquid light"; you should almost be able to see the fluid. Dip the end of a wand (or athame) into the cup as if it were a pen or brush. "Paint" with the wand or the athame on the surface of the shield, imagining that white, glowing lines are appearing on the shield and that they remain. Dip the wand or athame into the cup as often as the lines seem to dim. Sketch curves, circles, lines, etc., then "erase" the shield by slowly passing your hand across the surface. You may desire to start with the universal cross-circle (Celtic cross) symbol (⊕ or "earth and cosmos"), then letters, and finally words and pictures. You should be able to look away, then look back and see the writing still there. It should first be kept simple, to be vivid. After some practice, try "writing" in black on the white side of the shield. Afterward, practice writing in colors. This is quite important—practice often.

4.3 Projections—Sit at reading distance from the black shield, with the only light coming from a single candle placed behind you. Imagine that a beam of light projects pictures onto the shield from the center of your forehead. Picture various images as clearly as possible, starting with simple objects such as a butterfly, a bird, a person, and gradually working up to houses, street scenes, countryside, and moving scenes and people. Erase with a wand or athame. Practice frequently.

Repeat the above, but practice with three dimensional and solid projections. Erase with wand or athame.

4.4 Reception—Repeat the above, but let any image come of its accord. Note that the shield will fill with mist, brighten, and dark or bright images will appear. The images will be faint silhouettes at first, but become more vivid and detailed with practice. The shield may at times appear to you to be a window to Elsewhere; used in this manner, it truly is such a portal. You should note that some of the images you receive will be symbolic in nature, while others will be actual happenings, either past, present, or future. Erase the images with a wand or athame when needed. Very important, practice often.

4.5 Banishing—With the help of your imagination, visualize a small, common, and ugly or unaesthetic object on your floor. Take the shield and with black grease pencil or crayon, write "Peace" or "Relax" on the white side; with white grease pencil or crayon, write "Go" or "Depart" on the black side. Reinforce your image of the object on the floor; then hold up the pentacle with the black side toward the unwanted object, between you and the object. When you lower the shield, visualize and know that the object has been repelled beyond time and space. Repeat with another object. Important, practice frequently.

"Apprentice" Magical Training

According to the most ancient tradition, the four pillars of sacred Magic, and the four characteristics of one who would study it, are *Knowledge*, *Daring*, *Volition*, and *Silence*.

VISUALIZING A SOUND UNTIL IT IS HEARD

Imagine vividly a clock on the wall; see it just as though it were actually there. Watch the pendulum and listen to it tick. Repeat this visualization exercise, but with a person sounding a large gong; with a small brook, and listen to the sound of running water; with a pine forest, and listen to the wind in the treetops. Five minutes is the goal. Record your progress.

VISUALIZING A PLACE YOU KNOW WELL

Close your eyes and imagine *in full* some place you know, or have known quite well. Hold every detail quite vividly in your mind. Five minutes of undisturbed visualization is your goal. Record your progress.

VISUALIZING A PLACE YOU HAVE NEVER SEEN

Repeat the previous exercise, but with a locale you have never seen. Hold every stone and blade of grass clearly before your eyes. Five minutes is the goal. Record your progress.

ALL OF THE ABOVE EXERCISES, WITH EYES
FIRST CLOSED, THEN OPEN

Repeat each of the above exercises with your eyes open. Hold the scene so vividly that it seems to be a "fata morgana" superimposed on your true surroundings. Five minutes is the goal. Record your progress.

Repeat the above steps with farm animals and house pets. You should see their every movement, as in a cat washing itself, or a dog running about and barking. Five minutes is the goal. Record your progress.

Repeat the above with people, first with friends and relatives, then those deceased, strangers, adults and children, all races. Watch them working and listen to their voices. Five minutes at least. Record your progress.

Do not proceed until you have mastered, thoroughly all of the above.

PORE BREATHING WITH THE ELEMENTS

Inhale the fire element, breathing through all your pores. You should feel that as you inhale the "pressure" within yourself gets higher and higher, and that within yourself the heat is more and more intense. You are drawing the heat element from within the entire universe and building it within yourself. In the first exercise take in seven deep (but not restraining) breaths of fire element and hold them for a brief time, then breathe out the same number of breaths so that no fire element remains in your body. Each day, increase the number of breaths in this exercise by one, until you reach a maximum of twenty to thirty breaths. Only those with great willpower and physical strength should go beyond that. The beads from the previous exercises will be useful for counting your breaths. Record your progress.

Repeat the above with the air element, breathing through your pores. You should feel that your body is being filled like a balloon, and that you are getting lighter with each breath. Eventually you will not feel your body at all. Just as with the fire element, where the heat is real and can be measured with a thermometer, so also are the phenomena of the air element real. If intensely practiced for a long time, it would be possible with use of the air element to levitate, to walk on water, and to drift through the air. Again, start with the seven breaths on the first day, remembering to breathe out as many breaths as you take in, so not one particle of

air element remains within your body— otherwise there will be bad aftereffects. Each day, increase the number of breaths by one, until you reach twenty or thirty breaths. Again, your beads will be useful for counting. Record your progress.

Inhale the water element using pore breathing. You should feel as if your body is filling with cold water, and that you can feel the wetness of the element. By the time you have inhaled seven breaths of the element, you should feel as cold as ice, then return to normal as you breathe out seven breaths. History has shown that adepts who mastered this technique can create rainstorms, ban thunderstorms, calm the ocean, control creatures beneath the sea, and so on. With practice, you should be able to stay cool in the hottest weather with training in the water element. Start with seven breaths and work up to twenty or thirty, gradually, using your beads for counting. Record your progress.

Inhale the earth element using pore breathing. You should feel as if your body is filling with dense, heavy material which grows denser and heavier as you continue to inhale. Again, start with seven breaths and gradually build up to twenty or thirty, using your beads for counting. Record your progress.

Continuing practice of the preceding exercises will by now have given you greater willpower, better health, a better memory, and a clear intellect. You will find that you are improving in all ways, that you are developing unsuspected capabilities within yourself.

Using pore breathing, fill yourself strongly with akasha and hold it. You will experience intense pressure within yourself and feel that you are radiating like a small sun into the room about you. Press into the akasha and desire that all who enter the room will be at peace. Breathe out the vital force so that it will (by your command) stay in the room. Thus the room will be a very serene place, until you eventually release the akasha. This is a most valuable exercise, for with this exercise you can fill a room with an atmosphere conducive to work and intense study, or you can charge it so that unwelcome individuals will either feel vaguely uneasy and leave, or will be repulsed outright. You can seal your home and vehicle, or even that of a friend's, against theft and for safety. As the akasha knows neither time nor space, you can do this charging from a far distance. Or you can form the akasha into an astral "cloak of protection" about yourself or some other. The akasha's uses are very broad, but use them wisely! Practice very frequently.

BIOMAGNETISM

The akasha, or vital force, has the property of accepting any ideas or feelings impressed upon it, whether yours or another's. Thus, unless you include a proviso that "the effect will last thus-and-so long, and be unaffected by any others" it will tend to grow weaker after a time. Therefore, always include a time-sense.

The following rules apply:

- When working with the akasha principle, remember that it is timeless and spaceless.

- In the mental sphere one works and operates with time.

- In the astral sphere one works with space (shape and color).

- In the material world, one works with time and space simultaneously.

If as above, you wish to charge one room for a place of study and another room to be conducive to health and well-being, then do so, but do not attempt to mix the two. It is far better to charge each room for some particular activity.

LOADING OF A RING, JEWEL, OR TALISMAN

Fix the virtue you desire (luck, persuasion, love, etc.) into the ring, jewel, or talisman, concentrating that the wish and force will remain in the object forever, and even draw further force from the universe as soon as the object is used by the wearer. You can also do a "short-time" loading to accomplish some specific goal, and then allow the force to fade. If the Magically charged object is to help someone improve in some way, that person may be given the object, told what its purpose is, and told to recharge it by wearing, cleaning, or washing it at certain intervals.

"Universal loading" operates in the same way as the above, except for the concentrated wish that as long as the object (ring, stone, or jewelry) exists, the bearer will be benefitted by fortune, success, etc. Such a charge can last for centuries.

In both of the above cases the object should, of course, be heavily charged with akasha as you press in your wish.

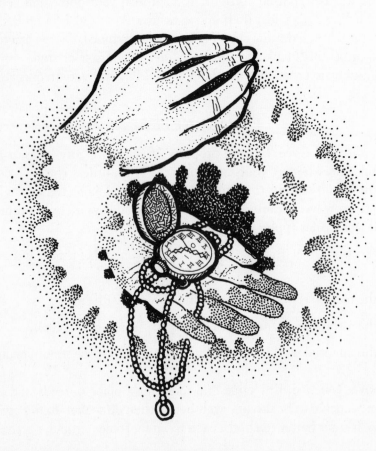

HEALING BY MAGIC, HERBS, OR
CONVENTIONAL MEDICINE

In Magical or psychic healing, the healer, with the aid of his or her imagination, makes vital force flow from his own body into that of a sick person. Generally the energy is transferred through the hands.

The "magnetizer" must above all be *completely* sound physically, and possess surplus vital force. He also must have excellent character, for he also transfers his own vibrations into the patient. Generally, in psychic healing, you draw the vital force from the universe and "stream" it consciously into the one who is sick. But always concentrate that the patient will be better and better, hour by hour, and day by day.

Know and study the diagnoses of diseases, study anatomy, and study medical literature extensively.

Infectious diseases or those requiring operations should by all means be left to conventional medicine. If there is no other choice, infectuous diseases can be treated by these methods or by "pulling off" at the auric area of the worst problem and the disease "thrown" into a living plant or washed down a drain. If one must do this, it is useful to wear silver bracelets and rings to keep the essence of the illness from extending beyond the hands. Then wash your hands and jewelry thoroughly in cold water afterward to clean away the left-over illness.

Keep in mind that modern medical science is extremely effective and should never be sold short.

Psychic healing can aid in the recovery from operations and for maladies which respond little or not at all to medicine, and can even frequently effect relief or cures of "incurable" illnesses. Migraines, allergies, stomach troubles, and illnesses which may have a psychosomatic origin respond very well to psychic healing.

A study of herbs used for healing is strongly recommended as a supplement to your practice of psychic healing.

The basic guidelines of psychic healing are as follows.

- Before approaching the sick person draw at least seven breaths of vital force from the universe and into your body through the pores.

- Let this vital force shine out through you like a sun.

- Try to produce radiant energy up to ten yards out, which would correspond to the vital energy of more than ten persons.

- You ought to feel that you are glowing with life-force. Your very nearness to a sick person will give relief.

- Transfer the energy through your hands or any way you want. A vivid and clear imagination is the important thing!

- With your willpower direct the compressed radiant energy to "stream" into the patient through his pores, and *will* that it will heal him.

There are three basic methods of psychic healing:

Healing Method #1

1. You must be convinced the patient is feeling better hourly and daily.

2. *Order* the radiant energy not to leave until the patient is recovered.

3. Load the subject with radiant energy so it is three feet from the body.

4. Repeat the loading after a while to increase the tension even more. In this way you can treat hundreds of patients without ruining your mental strength or your nerves.

Healing Method #2

1. Increase your radiant energy up to the ten-yard emitting radius.

2. The patient must be firmly convinced that he is inhaling your radiant energy with each breath, and that he is strengthening. He must believe the healing power will stay with him, and that he will be getting better and better.

If the patient cannot concentrate, or if the patient is a child, imagine yourself that the energy is being absorbed into the blood, and the healing is a continuous process, going on automatically.

Healing Method #3

1. Press the vital power "directly" into the patient's body, or into the sick organ or portion, through his or her pores.

2. "Will" the vital force to renew itself constantly from the universe until the recovery is complete.

This method is only practiced with patients whose nervous systems still possess some strength. It is the most popular method of healing.

An alternate method of healing would be to make contact with the mind and then to treat by the above means. Still another way would be to heal with the elements or with psychic electrical or magnetic force. Contact with the mind can be made while the patient is sleeping.

TRANSPLANTING OF CONSCIOUSNESS

Sitting in the asana position, fix your eyes on some everyday objects in front of you. Pick one of the objects and transplant your consciousness into it. Adopt all of its properties, its shape, its size, its function, etc. Practice this exercise until you can hold it for five minutes. Record your progress.

Repeat the above with bigger objects: flowers, plants, shrubs, trees, etc. Practice until you can hold it for five minutes. Record your progress.

Repeat the above with a dog, a cat, a horse, a bull, a deer, etc. See what the animal sees, feel what the animal feels, act as it acts. In this case you can work through the imagination entirely, and not see the animal at all. This exercise has an excellent result; it will deepen your understanding of our "little brothers." It also will enable you to handle any animal by your willpower. Used carefully with the technique of astral traveling, it can ultimately allow part of you to go out as a were-creature (but be guided by the Goddess!). Record your progress.

Repeat the above with people. Start with those who are well-known to you, then those lesser known, then strangers. Repeat with different ages, sexes, and races. Practice at least five minutes for each type. Record your progress.

CONCENTRATING ELEMENTAL ENERGY INTO ORGANS OR PARTS OF THE BODY

Sitting in the asana position, inhale with the lungs and pores, concentrating any element in one part of the body or one organ of the body. Remember to breathe out *exactly* the number of breaths of the element that you breathe in. Repeat with all the elements and all the major organs of the body. Never, however, should you attempt to concentrate any element in the brain or the heart. Practice "quick release," or "throwing" the accumulated element out with one gesture. Record your progress.

TRANSFERRING ALL YOUR CONSCIOUSNESS INTO ONE PART OF YOUR BODY

Transfer your consciousness and personality into one part of your body and allow it to inhale and concentrate one of the elements. Repeat with all of the elements. Start with seven breaths and work up to thirty. Record your progress.

THE IMPORTANCE OF NAMES

It is one of the most ancient principles of Magic that any thing or any creature not receiving and bearing a special name, symbol, or external mark is *without significance*. Also, not only can any idea be represented by a symbolic action, but it can be bound to a specific task or creature as well. These basic principles are most important in setting up any type of ritual.

"GESTURE" RITUALS

A small rite with considerable power can be set up using the relationship principles in the analogy chart that follows, gesturing with the fingers in a series of combinations to project the positive or negative aspects of the elements, and these forces aimed by the mind toward a certain goal.

Drawings of circles, mandalas, and other figures can be used, so long as you remember that such things are only "mental supports."

From the most ancient of times in far pre-history, Witches and Magicians have known that each of the five fingers in a series of combinations is particularly suited to act as a channel for one of the elements, through which the force can be projected (or else "misted") like water from a hose. Positive forces are better projected from the right hand, while negative forces are better projected from the left hand.

The Hand and the Analogy of the Elements

Forefinger	Fire
Thumb	Water
Middle finger	Akasha
Ring finger	Earth
Little finger	Air
The fingers of the right hand	Active elements
The fingers of the left hand	Negative elements

Further research into this area is strongly recommended, for these principles are reflected in palmistry, the Tarot, and in mythology. In Robert Graves' book, *The White Goddess*, ancient uses of these analogies in the Craft are shown, and the occult and spiritual consequences discussed. Assigning individual signs to different ideas will imbue each small ritual or set of gesticulations with its own meaning. Know that it will be successful! And finally, there is one other very basic principle. If you repeat any ritual frequently you will build up a rather strong reservoir of power which will last for a long time and will always be available to you. Any idea, every desire, and every imagination can be realized by a rite. Meditate and practice!

Master all of the preceding before going on to the next level of training.

~

"Journeyman" Magical Training

TRANSFERRING YOUR CONSCIOUSNESS INTO THE CENTERS OF OBJECTS

A so-called "depth point" exists at the center of any object, no matter how regular or irregular it may be. In the science of physics this is called the center of mass, or center of gravity, but the importance of this point Magically goes even far beyond known mechanics. The depth-point is at the nucleus, the starting point, the point of beginning of every form. Working at this point we have the key to the "fourth dimension," to time and space, to timelessness and spacelessness, and hence to the secret of space-Magic. Meditate and consider this for a while.

Take the asana position. (See illustration on page 210.) Put several symetrical objects in front of yourself: a ball, a die, an ellipsoid, etc. Close your eyes and transfer your consciousness into the center-point of one item. Make the transfer so complete that you forget about your body. Remember—while you are at the center point, you are at the center of all *dimensions*. When you have transferred yourself into the center-point, you should seem smaller and smaller, as small as a mustard seed or an atom, while the object should loom about you like a universe. Spend five minutes in each object. Record your progress.

Repeat the above with assymetrical objects. Record your progress.

Recognizing Component Material and Mental Structures, and Influencing Them

With practice in transferring your consciousness, you can gain the ability to look through any object and to intuitively recognize the material as well as the mental structure of any object. Also you can influence any object in its nucleus, to load it Magically at will, from the center outward.

209

Looking into the Centers of People and Animals

Practice the foregoing exercises with people, with animals, and with objects that are not nearby and which are out of sight. Record your progress.

Again, practice the above exercises, but this time transfer yourself into your own solar plexus. Remember, the smaller you can imagine yourself and the more you can forget about your body, the more successful the exercise. Five minutes is the goal. Record your progress.

CREATING MATERIAL MANIFESTATIONS
WITH THE ELEMENTS

Sitting in the asana position, inhale the fire element into your body. By imagination release it into the room where you are practicing. Repeat it again and again until you feel a perceptible warmth in the room. (This warmth is not imaginary; it can be measured with a thermometer.) You may even leave the room and it will remain loaded, but you should not allow the room to remain charged too long. Fire elementals will find it very "comfortable" and to their liking, and will eventually begin playing some of their pranks. (This is the basic technique used in an evocation: to charge an area so that it it will be comfortable to some elemental entity, and then to call the entity through a brief ceremony.) Practice until you are satisfied. Record your progress.

Repeat the above with the other elements. If you are working outside and have no walls to contain the elemental forces, be sure to "portion off" with your imagination some working place in your vicinity. Record your progress.

Repeat the accumulation exercise as before, but accumulate the element in one or both hands. Emit the element suddenly *by a motion of the hand*. Repeat this with all the elements, building up to thirty breaths of each. Practice frequently. Record your progress.

CREATING AND DISSIPATING BALLS AND
OTHER SHAPES OF THE ELEMENTS

Sit in the asana position and accumulate the fire element in your solar plexus in the shape of a ball four or six inches in diameter. It should glow within you like a tiny, hot sun. With a gentle motion of your hands, move the ball directly out through your solar plexus into the room, shining hot and bright. (With practice, an intense concentration such as this can actually light up a room.) With the help of your imagination, dissolve the ball slowly, or destroy it with a puff of breath.

Practice both means of dissipating the element-ball and repeat the exercise with all of the elements. Record your progress.

Repeat the above exercise, but shape the fire-element into a cone, a cube, a pyramid, or other configuration before moving it out from your body. Repeat with all the elements. Record your progress.

Fill your room with an intense concentration of the fire-element, inhaling it directly into the room rather than through your body. Then dissolve it. Repeat with all the elements. With practice it is possible to use the fire-element to keep a room warm in the winter. The water element will keep it cool in the summer. Record your progress.

Draw the fire-element in from the universe, concentrating it into a ball floating in the air just in front of you, without bringing it through your body. Dissolve it. Repeat with the other elements. Record your progress.

ONE METHOD OF STRIKING THE MAGICAL FLAME

As above, draw the fire-element into an intense fiery ball before you. Make it very strong and very intense. Compress it into a bead with your imagination, then into a spark. Add more fire-element and compress it again, repeating the process several times. Then guide the intensely hot spark into a cotton plug soaked with alcohol, and let it stay there. Then prepare a similar spark of the air-element. When you "touch" the air-spark to the cotton plug, it will catch fire. This technique can be used to light a candle. Fire and water thrown together into a tumbler will cause it to shatter; on a larger scale this multiple-element exercise can be used to produce lightning, thunder, rain, etc. Practice is important. Record your progress.

TASTING THE ELEMENTS

Obtain a jar of distilled water and a clean glass tumbler. Concentrate the fire-element into a half-filled glass of water and taste it; the water will taste somewhat acidic. Repeat with the water-element into another glass of water; it will have an astringent taste. With the earth-element it will taste musty. With the air-element it will taste sweet. Record your progress.

INITIAL LEVITATION EXERCISES

Passive means for communication with entities from the other planes, as given here, resemble Spiritualist techniques but allow you to maintain control and to direct your powers consciously, rather than being completely "taken over."

Sit in front of a table and put your hands on it. Accumulate akasha in your right hand and concentrate on the idea that with willpower alone—and no muscular effort whatsoever—you can control the hand. Diffuse away the vital power. Now concentrate the air-element very intensely in the forefinger of one hand, until the finger seems light as air. WILL the finger to lift, and have it do so, using no muscles. Then drop it and diffuse away the air-element. In this exercise, concentration is most important! Repeat with all the other fingers, then with the fingers of the other hand, then with each hand, and with each arm. This exercise is the key to such seeming miracles as walking on water or levitating through the air, and with considerable practice with all the parts of the body, you can accomplish this sort of thing. However, for our purposes here it is only necessary that you be able to raise and drop your fingers at will. Record your progress.

EXUDING THE SPIRITUAL OR PSYCHIC HAND
FROM THE PHYSICAL ONE

Sit at a table with your hands on the table top. Imagine that your spiritual hand is protruding from your right physical hand. Move the psychic hand about, being convinced that the psychic hand is the real hand. Return the psychic hand into the physical hand. Repeat with the left hand. Five minutes with each is the goal. Record your progress.

CONTACTING A SPIRIT GUIDE

Every person who works with things spiritual and psychic has, on the astral plane, a guide or teacher assigned to him or her. This guardian genius is in frequent contact with the subconscious, and does all he or she can do to aid you in your psychic development. Your guide is usually someone who has previously lived a number of lives upon the earth-plane. Contact with your guide, and with other disembodied entities, is possible through the following means.

USING A PENDULUM

Make a pendulum by tying a small weight such as a ring or stone to the end of a thirteen-inch string. A lady's pendant will work just as well. Hold the end of the string such that the pendulum swings freely about an inch above the table top, and with your elbow up and unsupported. Place your spirit hand at the disposal of your psychic guide, and do not let your physical hand either help or hinder the motion of the pendulum. Tell it to swing and indicate "yes," tell it to swing and indicate "no," and "maybe." Then ask any questions you want. Practice frequently.

Mark the letters A-Z across the top of a board or paper. Let the swinging of the pendulum spell out the words for you. Later, place a smooth sheet of glass over the board or paper, and use a small glass or tumbler, moved by the psychic hand, to spell out the messages. Practice frequently.

AUTOMATIC WRITING

You should cultivate the talent of automatic writing, as it can be useful to yourself and others. A good way to start would be to place your mind in a receptive condition and simply begin writing "free train of thought"—i.e., whatever comes to mind, without helping or hindering or even particularly thinking about it. After some practice, your talent will grow rapidly.

There are three types of automatic writing:

1. Automatic or mechanical: The hand writes absolutely automatically, without your knowing what information will be written or what will be given to you. This method can also give you paintings or messages in other languages.

2. Inspirational: It is as if you were "thinking" aloud inside or outside your own personality. The messages may come from the depths of your soul or from outside. You *know* what you will write.

3. Intuitive Method: You have the feeling that you did it yourself.

Practice frequently.

ASTRAL TRAVELING USING THE DREAM METHOD

You should have been keeping a listing of your dreams for some time now, and should have developed the capability to remember them quite well. If you have such a list, in the evening, just before you sleep, fix in your mind some place that you would like to visit, or some person that you would like to see. In your dreams *will* yourself to be wearing different clothes, or *will* yourself to suddenly be in some other locale. Practice very frequently. Record your progress.

"Master" Magical Training

FUNCTIONS OF THE MIND, CORRELATED WITH THE ELEMENTS

The functions of the mind in respect to the elements are as follow:

Will	Fire	Feeling	Water
Intellect Intelligence Memory	Air	Consciousness	Earth

Meditate on this and get a clear impression of each. It will enable you to control these functions in yourself and others.

IMAGING MENTAL AND ASTRAL BODIES WITHIN YOUR PHYSICAL BODY

Imagine your mental body, within your astral body, within your physical body, as though you were wearing a silk glove over your hand and a wool glove over that. Meditate on this. Take ten minutes. Record your progress.

Imagine that with any part of the physical body that moves, so also is the same part of the mental body moving, and also the same part of the astral body, each within the others. Meditate on this for ten minutes. Record your progress.

HUMAN OVERDRIVE: CHARGING THE MENTAL AND ASTRAL EQUIVALENTS OF YOUR BODY

Remember that any time you are magnetizing with your hands, or putting forth psychic energy with your hands or fingers in any way, the *physical, mental, and astral hands* must emanate simultaneously. Imagine that whatever you are seeing is being perceived not only by your physical eyes, but your mental eyes and astral eyes as well. Ten minutes. Record your progress.

Repeat the above exercise with hearing, sensing sound with your physical, mental, and astral ears simultaneously. It is especially rewarding to listen to music in this way. Ten minutes is the goal. Record your progress.

Repeat the above exercise with feeling. Ten minutes is the goal. Record your progress.

Repeat the above exercise with two senses simultaneously. Ten minutes is the goal. Record your progress.

UNITING WITH THE ETHER, AND THE ENTIRE UNIVERSE

Assume the asana position and close your eyes. Imagine that you are in the center of an unlimited space filled with the finest of matter, the universal ether (See illustration on page 218.). To your mental and astral senses it will appear to have an ultraviolet color. Inhale seven breaths of it and convey it into your bloodstream, then disperse it. Gradually increase to thirty breaths. Record your progress.

Repeat the above exercise, but fill the entire body. *You should feel united with the entire universe.* Record your progress.

CONTROLLING ALL THE ELEMENTS ON THE MENTAL, PHYSICAL AND ASTRAL PLANES

Using the akasha principle in this way you become united with the universe, yet secluded completely from the world. It is an unusual state of mind and an unusual state of being. This is the condition of those within a Witch's Circle or within any Circle you may make for special Magic. Any wish, any thought, any imagination created in this sphere, with the dynamic concentration of willpower, faith, and the fullest conviction is bound to be realized.

Sitting in the asana position, inhale the akasha and fill the whole body. As you inhale, *know* that you are initiating control of the four elements; they will fulfill anything that you order! Be confident! Record your progress.

Word and Gesture Rites for Controlling the Elements

Note that the elements can be projected on all planes, Mental, Physical, and Astral. The power of the elements can be directed by a suitable ritual, which you yourself can compose. You may use the finger-gestures, positions of hands, selected formulas or words, and the various elements drawn in and discharged from your body at various times during the ritual. Use logic and intuition in setting up a ritual, and you will surely be right!

To accomplish an objective, set up one ritual for an element of the astral sphere. Also compose a second ritual to dissolve this power almost immediately. Operate the same with the other three elements. When you have performed these eight power rites on the astral sphere, compose eight more for the mental sphere

and eight more for the material sphere. This is a difficult series of rites to accomplish, for full concentration must be maintained at all times. It is an extremely powerful form of Magic!

Remember, everything can be achieved! Practice, practice, practice!

You should be continuing with your previous exercises as a matter of habit, mastering them better and better as time goes on.

DELIBERATE CREATION OF ELEMENTALS

As a practitioner of Magic it is now within your power to create living beings: entities which at first will have their primary existence on the astral, but which will, with continuing use, start to appear on the physical plane. These beings can make excellent servants for you and for others, and you can create quite a number of them. Elementals can be of great use in influencing others' minds, in strengthening the intellect, in building friendships, in getting others to adopt your feelings and point of view, and to improve your own mind. There are many other uses, but you must always remember to use this power wisely and honestly. Remember also the basic rule among the Witches:

> *The good that ye do returns to you three times over … the evil that*
> *ye do also returns to you … three times over!*

Rules for the Creation of Elementals

1. Use your imagination to create a form. Think very intensely.

2. It must have a name!

3. Its task must be firmly impressed by willpower and imagination. Give your orders in the present tense when creating and commanding.

4. Determine in advance its exact span of life.

How to Create Elementals

Try a sample case:

1. Choose a lamp, ball, jewel, etc. in which to store your elemental between tasks.

2. Imagine, as you sit in the asana position, a large universal ocean of light. Shape with your mind an immense ball of light.

3. Compress and accumulate it until it is twelve to twenty inches in diameter. Fix in your mind that after each task is accomplished it will return and attach itself to the "storage object."

4. Impregnate this "sun ball" with your goal and desire for it.

5. Give it a suitable name that only you will know: "Lucis," for example.

6. Fix its exact date of death.

7. Give it orders. "You will work at the task I have set until it is accomplished (or until a given date). Then you will return. Go now."

8. It is advisable to recall the elemental and load it with light and power every few days.

"ACCIDENTALLY CREATED" BEINGS

You are already familiar with the natural elementals who inhabit the astral plane, and the artificial ones who are created Magically. There are others, however, which are bothersome and should be avoided or controlled. These include "Larvae" which are formed involuntarily by a strong physical excitement in the mental plane, and disappear when the excitement fades. They have no form, but that which is symbolic of their sources. "Phantoms" originate from daydream fantasies; they strengthen with continued repetition (such as a guilt or persecution complex, or an erotic fantasy). These can sometimes become even strong enough to be seen in daylight. "Phantasms" are animated representations of deceased people, caused by praising, mourning, tributes, etc. Frequently, these will impersonate the departed, and hence account for many poor or inaccurate "contacts" of spiritualists. All these entities have a strong instinct for self-preservation.

PSYCHIC CONDENSORS

Certain herbal and metallic combinations provide ready accumulators, or "condensors" of psychic forces. It is convenient to brew some of these and keep them available for needed Magic.

Simple Condensor

Bring two-tenths pint of distilled water to a rapid boil, then add two tablespoons of dried camomile flowers. Take from the heat and allow to cool. Filter into a very clean container and keep refrigerated. This is very easy to prepare and can be used for many purposes.

Ophthalmic Fire-Lotion

Bring one-half pint of distilled water to a rapid boil, then add two teaspoons of dried camomile flowers and one teaspoon of *Herba Euphrasia* (Eyebright). Take from heat and allow to cool, then decant into another clean container. Take a bunch of dried willow-switches and light them, then plunge the burning switches into the lotion: this will infuse the lotion with the fire element. Filter it into a saucer and put it in front of you. Load your body with nine breaths of fire-element and transfer it into the liquid. You may also charge it with the desire that it greatly improve your astral sight. Put the lotion in a clean container and keep under refrigeration.

Universal Condensor

A "universal condensor" can be made of lime tree flowers, cucumber skin, acacia leaves, cinnamon flowers, peppermint leaves, leaves of viola odorata, willow leaves, and tobacco, all brewed into a strong tea. For the time being you will not need this. Similar condensors can be made specifically for earth, air, fire, and water. Such legendary things as elixirs of youth and "cauldrons of wisdom" were extremely well-prepared condensor fluids.

Solid Condensor

A solid condensor can be prepared by mixing equal volumes of all the planetary metals in powder form: lead, tin, iron, gold, copper, brass, and silver, plus pulverized aloe resin, animal charcoal, and mineral coal. For the time being you will not need this, but for advanced workings (and if you can afford the gold and silver) you may wish to make up a small amount for insertion into a hollow wand or other application.

FURTHER MAGICAL DEVELOPMENT

Your training has progressed far by now. Still, bear in mind that it is very important to maintain both a Magical, balanced mind, and a healthy body. At this time you may want to begin specialized training to develop special capabilities within yourself (i.e., clairaudience, far-seeing, or sensing other people's—or other entities'—emotions and consciousness at a distance). To correct a weakness within yourself, or to work on special talents you wish to attain, consult this chart, then pick out exercises from the following pages for special practice.

Elements	Fire	Air	Water	Earth	Akasha
Senses	Eyes	Ears	Perception	Taste	All in all
Exercises in concentration, meditation	Optic	Acoustic	Emotional	Expanding of the consciousness	Realizing realities
Fundamental qualities of the mind	Will	Intellect	Feeling	Consciousness	Conscience

If you realize a weakness in yourself, concentrate on appropriate psychic exercises (utilizing the above), to bring yourself into balance.

"Wizard" Magical Training

MAGICAL CLAIRVOYANCE DEVELOPMENT

Place a cotton pad soaked with the ophthalmic fire-lotion over each eye and rig a blindfold to hold the pads in place. Sitting in the asana position (see illustration, page 224), breathe in the Universal White Light which permeates everything. *Know* that you can see every place, everywhere that this light permeates. Concentrate this light in both eyes. Hold for ten minutes as you practice looking far beyond and about you. Then discharge and remove the pads. This exercise aids in using the crystal, the Magic-mirror, dark surfaces etc., for scrying, and improves your ability to understand any writing seen physically and astrally. Record your observations.

DEVELOPMENT OF ASTRAL CLAIRAUDIENCE

Practice of this exercise enables one to hear voices at the remotest distances and to understand the languages of all beings. Make up two new cotton plugs and moisten them with the simple condensor. Place them before you and imbue each with nine breaths of the air element. Insert the plugs into your ears and fill your head with nine breaths of akasha. Transfer your consciousness into the region of your ears. *Know* that you can hear anything, anywhere, absolutely! Discharge the akasha after at least ten minutes, and remove the plugs. Record your observations.

DEVELOPMENT OF ASTRAL CLAIRFEELING

This is the faculty of perceiving and feeling all the phenomena and powers occuring in the elements and everywhere that the akasha pervades. Practice if this exercise will develop you, capability for psychometry, materializations, sense perceptions and touch sensations.

Referring to your charts on your personality, strengths and weaknesses from page 222, note whether your personality is predominantly earth, air, fire, or water, and check below to note where you will place your pad of fluid condensor for this exercise.

- If the fire element is dominant, your astral sensory center: forehead.

- If the air element is dominant, your astral sensory center: heart.

- If the water element is dominant, your astral sensory center: solar plexus.

- If the earth element is dominant, your astral sensory center: hands or thighs.

Make a cotton pad, and moisten it with a condensor. Place it before you and imbue it with nine breaths of the water element. Lie on a couch and place the pad over the astral sensory area; keep your eyes closed from here on. Accumulate the water element into your body, picturing that you are floating in the Universal Water Element, in an endless ocean which pervades everywhere. Transfer your consciousness into the sensory area. Imagine intensely the strong magnetic power of the water. After at least ten minutes, gradually drop imagination of the universal water, dissolve the water element, remove and discharge the condensor pad. As you strengthen in this exercise you will be able, ultimately, to induce this faculty merely by transferring consciousness into the astral sensory area. Record your observations.

METHODS FOR CREATING ELEMENTARIES

An "elemental" is produced on the base of deliberate thoughts, and works mainly on the mental plane. An "elementary" is far more penetrating and subtle, and is created from one or several elements.

An elementary should only be given one task at a time, otherwise it may become confused. It must be made of elements suitable for the job, and it must be given a name at the moment of creation. The greater the loading, the better the elementary. Always keep them under control; otherwise you might become responsible karmically for a vampire!

Elementaries manufactured for your own use can be created through your own body, but those destined for use by others should be created by projection of the elements directly from the earth. You should fix the method for calling up an elementary at the time it is created.

There are two fundamental methods for creation of elementaries.

- Method #1: Projection of one element into a ready-made form.

- Method #2: Projection of several elements into a ready-made form.

Method #1 for Producing an Elementary

1. Place the "form object" before you; a lamp, ball, ring, etc. will do.

2. Fill the form object with the element appropriate to its task. Repeat again and again for a strong response.

3. Impregnate the doll with your desire for accomplishing the task.

4. Simultaneously, give it a name.

5. Simultaneously, allot it a lifetime.

6. Draw the elementary out and send it on its way to the task, ordering it to return "home" when it is finished with its task.

7. After sending the elementary off, *forget about it!* Otherwise, your thoughts may interfere with its work.

8. When you think the job might be accomplished, use a pendulum to check whether your elementary has returned. You can call it back for reloading.

9. When the elementary is back in the form object you may wrap the object in black silk, as silk is a psychic insulator. However, if you wrap the object when the elementary is away it will not be able to return and will die. This method will suffice if the job to be accomplished is a simple one. If not, you need a more complex elementary.

Method #2 for Producing an Elementary

1. Make a doll at least four inches high from two parts loam and one part beeswax.

2. Drive a pencil from its head to its feet to make a hollow opening.

3. Fill the hollow with a liquid condensor. If, *and only if,* the elementary is for personal use, add a bit of your own sperm or blood.

4. Seal the opening with wax.

5. Hold the doll in your left hand, and rub it gently with your right hand. Breathe into it and name it.

6. Through the doll's feet load the genital region with earth element and fix. Through its feet load the abdominal region with the water element and fix. Through its feet load the chest region with the air element and fix. Through its feet load the head region with the fire element and fix. The astral body has now been produced.

7. Concentrate into the doll's head the mental qualities that you want it to have.

8. Hold the doll in your left hand and accumulate a heavy charge of light from the universe in the right hand.

9. Fix the elementary's death date in your mind.

10. Transfer the light into the doll. Call it by its name. (You will begin to sense and feel its heartbeat and respiration.) Tell it joyously to *live.*

11. You may wrap the doll in black silk for storage, but *do not* wrap it when the elementary's astral is away, as this could kill it.

12. Allow no one else to touch it. Store it securely and safely.

13. Its size and clothing will be as you determine for each mission. The elementary will develop in size and potency as it is used. Be sure you remember your Utilization and Charging Ritual.

STORING THE ELEMENTARY'S ESSENCE IN A TIBETAN KYLICHORE

Method #1

1. Decide purpose, form, sex, name, life span, ritual for calling, and whether the elemental is to be bound to a doll or a talisman. Determine the storage location; it must not come into contact with strangers.

2. Draw a large circle on a piece of paper, and inscribe two squares within it, making an eight-pointed star which symbolizes both the positive and the negative aspects of all the elements. Draw a sign representing the elementary in the middle of the octogram. The elementary will stand at this spot. (See illustration on page 228.)

3. Engrave the same sign on a round piece of metal about one half inch in diameter. We now have the great Kylichore and the small Kylichore (Kylichore: a place for storage and preservation of the elementary). Place the small Kylichore in the center of the great Kylichore.

4. Call the elementary by the name you have chosen, bearing in mind all of Step 1 above.

5. Assuming that this is a flame elementary, sit in the asana position and inhale the fire element, impregnating it with your desire. (Animate it afterward with your imagination.) Transfer the accumulated fire element into the center of the small Kylichore. Repeat this again and again; a spark will begin to grow.

6. When you grow tired, send the elemental off to its storage place in a section of wall, a doll, or a talisman, for instance. Put the small Kylichore in a safe place, fold the large one and put it away.

7. When you want to continue charging, spread put the great Kylichore, place the small one in the center and call the elementary's name. And the flame will reappear. Continue as before, frequently adding to the flame.

8. When it is large enough, transmute the flame into the desired shape. Even then, you can continue loading it. (The large Kylichore is used only for loading.)

9. To use the elementary, utilize the ritual or take the small Kylichore in hand and give an order.

Method #2 — Advanced Tibetan Method.

Same as Method #1 (beginning on page 227), but imagine the complete shape from the beginning.

MAGICAL ANIMATION OF PICTURES

Cut a piece of blotting paper or cardboard to the size of the picture.

1. Moisten the paper with the fluid condensor and let it dry. If the picture is an oil painting, the condensor is not required.

2. Place the paper directly against the back of the picture and protect it from dust.

3. As in Method #2 for Producing an Elementary (page 226), form the mental body by imagination. It must correspond to the size of the picture. If

the picture does not show the whole figure, then fill in what is missing with your imagination. Transfer the desired mental capabilities.

4. Project the elements as indicated in Method #2.

5. Call it to life as in Method #2.

6. It is often advisable to store the elementary in the wall *behind* the picture. Otherwise, your visitors will begin seeing the image move as it gets stronger, and you may pick up an unfortunate reputation.

7. The same method applies to statues and busts.

It is not advisable to animate pictures with great sexual appeal because the elementary could possibly come to control *you*.

DISSOLUTION OF ELEMENTARIES

Dissolution Process #1

If you give your elementary a pre-set death date there should be no problem in having it last too long. However, if you want to deactivate it ahead of time, the following technique should be used.

1. Holding the doll in the left hand, load your right hand very heavily with akasha, so that it glows blue-black.

2. Project akasha, suddenly, into the heart of the doll to stop its heart and lungs.

3. Remove and dissolve the mental body into the Universal Light. This dissolves the elementary's mental body.

4. Dissolve each element of its astral body, one at a time.

5. Break off its head, catch any condensor fluid in a blotter, and burn it.

6. Bury the waxen figure in some remote location.

Dissolution Process #2

If your elementary is very strong the following method should be used.

1. Fill your bathtub with water as hot as you can stand. Get in.

2. Hold the figure, wrapped in silk, in your left hand.

3. Load your right hand very heavily with akasha.

4. Shake off the silk wrapping with the left hand, immediately kill the elementary with an akasha bolt, and submerge the doll in the tub.

5. Think intensely that all power, all abilities, all life is passing through the water into your body, soul, and mind.

6. Any excess remaining power remains in the water and protects you from "Magical backlash."

7. Get out of the tub and dry off, leaving the doll in the cooling water. Drain the water. If the doll still has an aura, fill the tub with hot water again, and let the doll soak for a little longer.

8. Burn or bury the silk wrapping and the remains of the doll.

More Training

Yes, much more training is possible. If you've mastered all of it up through "Wizard," a five-year task at the very least, then contact me through the publisher, if you want. Let's talk.

All of this is likely to take quite a while, and by the time you finish with it, you probably will know quite well where you want to study and progress next. Just remember:

> It is not just the final goal,
> But the journey itself,
> Which is worthy and memorable.
> For the adventures of the mind,
> The spirit, and the soul
> Which one encounters in the Quest
> Are enriching beyond all measure.
> And, so, worthy seeker,
> Go ever in the Way of the Gods
> And know Their blessings!

> Blessed Be,
> Ed Fitch

CONCLUSION

TO THOSE OF THE "INNER COURT"

The "Book of Shadows of the Outer Court" and the "Grimoire of Shadows" are companion volumes to be used in setting up Outer Court (or training) covens. Insofar as was possible, all rites and practices have been drawn from traditions, folklore, and historical sources and have reasonably good accuracy. The method of Magic employed, however, is usually between the ceremonial and Wiccan types.

One reason dictated the use of an oftimes relatively complex ceremonial method over always using the elegantly simple Witch Magic. Many of the ancient rituals, if entirely reconstructed according to Craft practice, end up being uncomfortably close to some existing rites. This, as any Wiccan knows, is no accident.

The exercises themselves give a good training in Magical thinking that will serve very well, no matter what the seeker's inclinations. A Magic-oriented inquirer would be led by Outer Court devotional rites to a new and greater reverence for the Lady.

There are several applications for an Outer Court. A version of it may be used by an already-established tradition to fill in any "holes" that it might have in its own ritual and training compendium. It may be used as a nearly or completely self-sufficient "front organization" to screen and train prospective initiates. Risks may be taken and new ground broken by an Outer Court organization, and initiates of proven high caliber may be obtained at will from Outer Court covens.

Also, the Outer Court is itself a complete, self-contained system.

Each group receiving this Outer Court material may add to, alter, and/or subtract from it depending on their respective branch of the Craft, their interests and desires, and local needs. The material, although parallel to Gardnerian Witchcraft, can be reconfigured to Celtic, Traditional, Latin, or Middle European types. Conceivably, it would even be possible to modify the Outer Court material to such variations as Mexican-Aztec, Ancient Egyptian, Mesopotamian, Grecian, a form of Norse Odinism, or even Polynesian Witchcraft. The only requirement, of course, would be that the basic traditions of the Craft not be altered.

A variety of rituals and traditions from many sources will give strength to an Outer Court movement, and to Wicca in general. Modifications and additions to this material are encouraged.

GLOSSARY

AKASHA: Magical life-force.

ANIMA: The female side of one's character.

ANIMUS: The male side of one's character.

ASPERGILLIS: A sprinkler for holy or consecrated water.

ATHAME: The Witch's traditional Magical tool, the consecrated, black-handled dagger.

BELTANE: May Eve or May first. One of the high festivals of Paganism.

BOOK OF SHADOWS: A compendium of Wicca rituals, spells, training techniques, procedures, guidelines, and other materials deemed important to a Witch or to a full coven. There is a wide variety of these books extant, most of which have not been published, as they are usually considered secret. Each Wicca tradition is likely to have its own more or less standard Book of Shadows.

BRASSARID: Devotee, Priestess, supporter. (Archaic poetic use.)

BRAZIER: Incense burner, or thurible. Usually ceramic or metal and often designed to be suspended or swung by a chain. Often they have a layer of sand in the bottom so that incense sticks may be inserted, or glowing charcoal briquettes are placed inside to be sprinkled with powdered incense.

CENSE, CENSER: see "Brazier."

CONDENSER, PSYCHIC: An herbal, mineral, or metallic substance which accumulates and holds Magical power.

CONSECRATION: Imbuing an object or substance with Magical power.

COVENSTEAD: The place, usually a residence, at which a coven regularly performs its rituals. In ancient times this would have been a temple.

CREATRIX: Female creator. Goddess.

CROSS-QUARTER DAYS: The traditional Pagan holidays which occur exactly between each Sabbat (q.v.) or Seasonal Festival (q.v.). These are Lady Day or Candlemas (February 2), Beltane (May 1), Lammas (August 1), and Samhain or Halloween (October 31).

CTHONIC: Of or pertaining to the depths of the Earth. There seem to be powerful cthonic Magical or psychic forces which are a part of the structure of each planet.

DANCE, MAGICAL: Any kind of dance can be for Magical purposes, so long as the goal is firmly fixed in the mind of the dancer(s) and any observers. In a coven, a commonly-used "ceremonial dance" is one in which the members of a coven will link hands and move clockwise within the ceremonial area. The basic "grapevine" circle step is "right foot cross over, left foot sidestep, right foot cross back, left foot sidestep," etc. It is free-form, with whirls, leaps, chanting, singing, and whatever else is desired.

DEDICATION: Generally, a resolution which one ritually makes before the Gods and before fellow Pagans that one intends to follow the Old Ways.

DEOSIL: Clockwise or sunwise, the standard way of moving within a ritual area or consecrated Circle.

DOLMEN: A standing, upright stone of the kind used in very ancient rituals throughout Europe and Britain.

ELEMENTALS: Magically or naturally created beings which have sentience and frequently intelligence. These include gnomes (earth), sylphs (air), undines (water), salamanders (fire), plus a great number of nature elementals such as fairies, leprechauns, tree maidens, dragons, etc. Artificial elementals can be created in almost any form.

ELEMENTS, MAGICAL: The Magical and spiritual equivalents of earth, air, fire, and water, each having a wide variety of subtle meanings and implications.

EQUINOXES: The two times of the year when the days and nights are of equal length: Spring (March 21, approximately) and Autumn (September 21, approximately). These are two of the Pagan high holidays (q.v.).

ESBAT: A Pagan or Wicca ceremonial time held usually between the high holidays (q.v.) and cross-quarter days (q.v.). Usually a full-moon rite.

GAUL: During the Roman Empire, the area now known as France.

GLYPH: Sacred or Magical symbol.

GRIMOIRE: Book of Magical workings or spells.

HAME: home (ancient term).

HANDFAST: marry.

HENGE: A sacred enclosure for outdoor rituals, usually made of stone, though occasionally of large wooden markers.

INITIATION: A ritual in which the individual is accepted into a higher ranking, reflecting a greater level of understanding and knowledge, before her or his coven members and before the Gods.

KHITON: Short, simple tunic of ancient Grecian design, often used in dancing rites.

KI: Oriental term for "life force" or akasha.

LABRYS: The sacred double-headed axe of ancient Crete, which is thought to have symbolized the Gods' thunderbolt and also was possibly an instrument for accumulating Magical power.

LEFT-HAND PATH: Using the Magical and metaphysical studies for evil ends.

OGHAM: The ancient Celtic "Tree Alphabet." See the writings of Robert Graves for in-depth explanations.

OLD RELIGION: Witchcraft and Paganism. So-called because they are, either by lineage or spiritually, a system of belief which existed long before the Judeo-Christian-Islamic religions.

PENTACLE, PANTACLE: The ceremonial tool on the altar which symbolizes Earth. It is usually round and either inscribed with a Pentagram and symbols pertaining to the Gods, or black on one side and white on the other. It is equivalent to both a shield and a Magic mirror.

PENTAGRAM: A traditional symbol of the five-pointed star, used as protection, or for invoking or banishing of Magical forces and entities. Symbolic of humankind made perfect, with many metaphysical meanings.

REDE: Rule or creed.

RIGHT-HAND PATH: Using the Magical and metaphysical studies for constructive ends.

RUNE: The ancient Norse alphabet. Also, any Magic spell of the old Norse.

SABBAT: The high holidays and cross-quarter days which are the traditional Wicca sabbats.

SAIN: Bless.

SCORE: Twenty.

SCRY: To seek images or symbols for guidance in the future or to explain something in the past. There is a very great variety of such means of divination: Tarot, crystal, pendulum, runestaves, channeling, etc.

SIGIL: Sacred or Magical symbol.

SPELL: A way of working some type of Magic; to make things happen by paranormal means.

SPRITES: The small, animated figures which sometimes are the visible manifestations of elemental beings.

SUMMERLAND: The paradisial "land between lives" of Wicca, where souls rest between reincarnations. It has many names in many religious systems.

SUNWARDS, SUNWISE: Clockwise or deosil (q.v.).

SUN WHEEL: The eight-spoked wheel has been the symbol of the year, the symbol of gaining wisdom through one's lifetime, and thus a symbol of the Gods, since far prehistoric times in the Northern European and Celtic lands.

THURIBLE: incense burner

"TIME OF THE BURNINGS": The times in Medieval and Rennaissance Europe and Britain when the Old Religion was persecuted by the Christian church. An estimated nine million followers of the Old Ways, and those alleged to be with them, died during these centuries.

TUATHA DE DAMNU, TUATHA DE DANAAN: Some of the legendary races which are said to have preceded the human race.

WICCA: Old Saxon word meaning "Magic worker," now used as a synonym for Witchcraft or Old Religion

WIDDERSHINS: To move counterclockwise within a ceremonial area or other ritual area. This is usually indicative of Chaos, and thus is considered to be bad practice.

STAY IN TOUCH...

LLEWELLYN PUBLISHES HUNDREDS OF BOOKS ON YOUR FAVORITE SUBJECTS

On the following pages you will find listed some books now available on related subjects. Your local bookstore stocks most of these and will stock new Llewellyn titles as they become available. We urge your patronage.

Order by Phone

Call toll-free within the U.S. and Canada, 1-800-THE MOON. In Minnesota call (612) 291–1970. We accept Visa, MasterCard, and American Express.

Order by Mail

Send the full price of your order (MN residents add 7% sales tax) in U.S. funds to:

Llewellyn Worldwide,

P.O Box 64383, Dept. K–605–X

St. Paul, MN 55164–0383, U.S.A.

Postage and Handling
- $4.00 for orders $15.00 and under
- $5.00 for orders over $15.00
- No charge for orders over $100.00

We ship UPS in the continental United States. We cannot ship to P.O. boxes. Orders shipped to Alaska, Hawaii, Canada, Mexico, and Puerto Rico will be sent first-class mail.

International orders: Airmail—add amount for freight equal to price of each book to the total price of order, plus $%.00 for each non-book item (audiotapes, etc.).

Surface mail: Add $1.00 per item

Allow 4–6 weeks delivery on all orders. Postage and handling rates subject to change.

Discounts

We offer a 20% quantity discount to group leaders or agents. You must order a minimum of 5 copies of the same book to get our special quantity price.

Free Catalogue

Get a Free copy of our color catalogue, *New Worlds of Mind and Spirit*. Subscribe for just $10.00 in the United States and Canada ($20.00 overseas, first class mail). Many bookstores carry New Worlds—ask for it!

MAGICAL RITES FROM THE CRYSTAL WELL
Ed Fitch

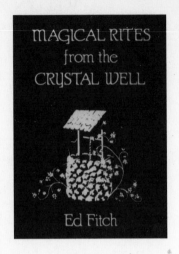

In nature, and in the earth, we look and find beauty. Within ourselves we find a well from which we may draw truth and knowledge. And when we draw from this well, we rediscover that we are all children of the Earth.

The simple rites in this book are presented to you as a means of finding your own way back to nature; for discovering and experiencing the beauty and the Magic of unity with the source. These are the celebrations of the seasons; at the same time they are rites by which we attune ourselves to the flow of the force: the energy of life.

These are rites of passage by which we celebrate the major transitions we all experience in life. Here are the Old Ways, but they are also the Ways for Today.

0-87542-230-6, 160 pp., 7 x 10, illus., softcover $12.95

THE RITES OF ODIN
Ed Fitch

The ancient Northern Europeans knew a rough Magic drawn from the grandeur of vast mountains and deep forests, of rolling oceans and thundering storms. Their rites and beliefs sustained the Vikings, accompanying them to the New World and to the Steppes of Central Asia. Now, for the first time, this Magic system is brought compellingly into the present by author Ed Fitch.

This is a complete source volume on Odinism. It stresses the ancient values as well as the Magic and myth of this way of life. The author researched his material in Scandinavia and Germany, and drew from anthropological and historical sources in Eastern and Central Europe.

A full cycle of ritual is provided, with rites of passage, Magical spells, divination techniques, and three sets of seasonal rituals: solitary, group and family. *The Rites of Odin* also contains extensive "how-to" sections on planning and conducting Odinist ceremonies, including preparation of ceremonial implements and the setting up of ritual areas. Each section is designed to stand alone for easier reading and for quick reference. A bibliography is provided for those who wish to pursue the historical and anthropological roots of Odinism further.

0-87542-224-1, 360 pp., 6 x 9, illus., softcover $14.95